ALSO BY JIM GRANT, BOB JOHNSON AND IRV RICHARDSON

The Looping Handbook:
Teachers and Students Progressing Together

Multiage Q & A: 101 Practical Answers to
Your Most Pressing Questions

BY JIM GRANT AND BOB JOHNSON

A Common Sense Guide to Multiage Practices

BY JIM GRANT

Retention and Its Prevention:
Making Informed Decisions About Individual Children

"I Hate School!"

Developmental Education in the 1990's

Every Parent's Owner's Manuals
(Three-, Four-, Five-, Six-, Seven-Year-Old)
(with Margot Azen)

Jim Grant's Book of Parent Pages

BY CHAR FORSTEN

The Multiyear Lesson Plan Book

Teaching Thinking and Problem Solving in Math (Scholastic)

Using Calculators Is Easy (Scholastic)

Our special gift to help you,
The ultimate change agent

Feel free to reproduce any of the pages of this book,
for educational purposes, within your school.

(Not to be distributed for use between schools
or throughout school districts.)

LOOPING

Q&A

72 Practical Answers to Your Most Pressing Questions

WRITTEN BY
CHAR FORSTEN
JIM GRANT
BOB JOHNSON
IRV RICHARDSON

Crystal Springs Books · Peterborough, New Hampshire

© 1997 by Char Forsten, Jim Grant, Bob Johnson and Irv Richardson
Printed in the United States of America

Published by Crystal Springs Books
Ten Sharon Road
PO Box 500
Peterborough, New Hampshire 03458
1-800-321-0401
FAX: 1-800-337-9929

Cataloging-in-Publication Data

Forsten, Char, 1948-
       Looping Q & A : 72 practical answers to your most pressing questions /
written by Char Forsten, Jim Grant, Bob Johnson, Irv Richardson. — 1st ed.
[128] p. : cm.
Includes bibliography, charts and index.
Summary : An easy to read question and answer book which describes multiyear
teaching and its benefits. Includes questions parents ask most, problems, and
implementation strategies.
ISBN : 1-884548-16-4
1. Teaching. 2. Learning. 3. Nongraded schools—Miscellanea. 4. Team learning
approach in education. I. Forsten, Char, 1948- . II. Grant, Jim, 1942- . III. Johnson, Bob, 1942- .
IV. Richardson, Irv, 1956- . V. Title.
371.2 '54—dc20   1997   CIP
LC Card Number: 96-67532

Editor: Aldene Fredenburg
Book and Cover Design: Susan Dunholter

Publishing Manager: Lorraine Walker
Production Coordinator: Christine Landry

For Lorraine Walker, whose creative spirit, leadership qualities, and "can-do" attitude have been the source of inspiration not only for Crystal Springs Books, but for all of us who work with her.

Acknowledgments

We have many people to thank:

Judy Boniface of Woodinville, Washington, whose experience in combining the multiage and looping concepts expanded our vision;

Daniel Burke, superintendent of the Antioch, Illinois, school system, whose exploration into interbuilding looping opened the benefits of looping up to a whole new group of children;

Bernie Hanlon, superintendent of the year-round Raisin City and West Park, California, school districts, who commented favorably on the compatibility of looping and year-round schooling;

Ted Thibodeau, assistant superintendent, and Dr. Joseph Rappa, superintendent of the Attleboro, Massachusetts, school district, who, along with their time, have provided much of the solid statistical data which supports looping; and the many teachers and principals of the Attleboro School District who shared their time and their knowledge with us;

Elizabeth Jankowski, whose doctoral dissertation provided valuable documentation on the success of looping in the Hilton Head school system.

In our own family at The Society For Developmental Education: Gretchen Goodman, who provided valuable information on special-needs students; and Yvette Zgonc, whose expertise on difficult children is also very valuable as well as compassionate;

Susan Dunholter, whose book design has contributed greatly to our presentation of this information;

Christine Landry, production coordinator, whose expertise in typesetting and dedication in meeting difficult deadlines has made this book happen in record time;

Aldene Fredenburg, our editor, whose patience in pulling together lots of disparate information and making it whole is always appreciated.

*C*ontents

What Is Looping, and What Are Its Benefits?

Q.

What is looping?

A. Looping is a practice which allows single-grade teachers to remain with the same class for a period of two or more years. It generally requires a partnership of two teachers in contiguous grades; a first-grade teacher, for instance, decides to progress with her students to grade two, while the second-grade teacher moves to first grade and begins a new two-year cycle.

CLASSROOM B
Second Year
Grade Level 2

CLASSROOM A
First Year
Grade Level 1

The concept of looping is not new. In 1913, the Department of the Interior recommended this same practice, but referred to it as "teacher retention." Since then, other terms have been used to describe looping, including: teacher-student progression; two-cycle teaching; multiyear teaching; and the twenty-month classroom (see page 30).

No matter what its name, the practice is the same. In a looping classroom, the teacher is the heart and the students are the focus.

Q.

What are the benefits of looping?

A. Looping is a very simple concept, but with profound benefits. Dr. Joseph Rappa, Superintendent of the Attleboro School District in Massachusetts, reports that students who have the same teacher for two years tend to enjoy school more, have fewer discipline problems, fewer absences, are referred to special education placement less often, and are less apt to be retained in a grade for lack of academic achievement.*

At the heart of a successful looping classroom are the continuity of relationship and the learning environment. Many of today's children are on a fast track along with their families, moving from home to school, to after-school activities, to day care, adapting to parents' job schedules along the way. Additionally, many children come from single-parent homes. Many children today lack continuity in their lives. Often the five-and-a-half hour period that children spend in school is the most stable and predictable part of their day. Keeping children with the same caring, concerned teacher over a two-year period provides the stable foundation that many children need.

Looping allows a teacher and children to get to know one another. Children learn the expectations of their teacher, while the teacher gets to know the needs and the strengths of individual students over this two-year period. The extended relationship gives the teacher time to respond to problems, academic or otherwise, that a child may have. With the additional year, teachers can focus more on learning, rather than "covering" the curriculum.

The looping classroom is time-efficient. Built into the looping relationship is extra time; most teachers find that their students start the second year of class as if it were the 181st day of school, needing virtually no period of adjustment before getting into the swing of learning. Teachers estimate that they gain at least a solid month of instructional time at the beginning of the second year of a looping cycle.

Teachers also have a head start in the second year with their relationships with parents. Bonds formed in the first year are strengthened during the second year. Many teachers report strong,

---

* Grant, Jim; Richardson, Irv; and Johnson, Bob. *The Looping Handbook: Teachers and Students Progressing Together.* Peterborough, NH: Crystal Springs Books, 1996, p. 15.

lasting friendships with the parents of children in a multiyear class (see page 46).

Discipline is much better in a looping classroom. By the second year of a two-year classroom, children know what is expected of them. They know the classroom routines and trust that they're in a consistent, stable environment. They've developed strong ties with their classmates and respond to positive peer modeling and peer pressure. Many teachers report that discipline problems drop dramatically in the second year of a multiyear arrangement.

The strong parent-teacher relationship that tends to form in a looping situation lets the child know that the teacher and parents are working together for his or her best interests. Also, the strong parental involvement that often accompanies a looping arrangement gives the child a sense of well-being that makes "acting out" less of an emotional necessity.

Student attendance tends to improve in a looping classroom. By the second year, teacher and students know what to expect from each other, and many strong friendships have been forged. With this sense of relationship and belonging, children want to come to school. Parents and teachers report fewer tummyaches, fewer lost gloves and shoes, and generally more enthusiasm for school. In Attleboro, Massachusetts, student attendance in grades two through eight has increased from 92% ADA to 97.2% ADA.*

Many of the instructional strategies that multiyear teachers find successful — thematic teaching, cooperative learning, learning centers, among others — make the looping classroom a place where children want to be.

Looping tends to reduce special education referrals. The two-year classroom gives children a longer academic runway. In a single-grade, single-year classroom, the teacher keeps a worried eye on the child who is not up to par as he nears the end of the school year. The looping teacher knows she has more time to work with the child before making such a high-stakes decision as a special education referral. The extra instructional time provided by the looping structure may be just enough to put many children over the top academically.

The looping arrangement also provides greater opportunity to observe children and determine their needs, and to better match the curriculum to those needs. A looping teacher can often devise effec-

---

* *The Looping Handbook*, p. 15

tive strategies the second year which are based on numerous observations from the previous year.

A growing concern among educators is that too many children are being referred for special education for academic problems that may simply reflect a normal variance in the rate at which children learn. Looping takes much of the time pressure off the teacher and reduces the chance of unnecessary referrals.

That being said, we must remind people that looping is not a substitute for special education. While it will provide many children with the extra time and support they need, it will not in and of itself resolve learning disabilities, and it will not end the need for adaptations due to physical disabilities. There is a danger that, given the forgiving nature of the looping classroom, a child may miss being referred to special ed services that she may need (see page 69).

One alarming development is that some states are considering capping the number of children allowed to receive special education services. This is a response to the extremely high cost of providing federally mandated special education services. If these caps are allowed to be created, school systems will find themselves doing triage on their students; looping may optimize the time spent in the regular classroom for those students who no longer qualify for special ed services. (See pages 19, 65, and 69-70 for further discussions of special education and looping.)

Looping reduces (but does not eliminate) grade level retentions.
When teachers have children for two years, they don't have to make retention decisions at the end of the first year, because that barrier no longer exists. The teacher can use the two-year span to help bring children up to grade level academically.

Often, children who are lagging behind don't need to repeat an entire grade; they just need a little more time to better understand concepts. With the extra learning time provided in the beginning of the second year, and with the teacher's increased understanding of the child's needs, strengths, and weaknesses, the trauma of grade-level retention often isn't necessary.

Sometimes, a child's lagging abilities may not be so much an academic problem as a problem of readiness. If a child, especially a kindergarten or first-grade child, is developmentally young, retention may be the appropriate solution (see pages 93-94 and 104-107).

Q.

Are some educators making looping sound too complicated?

A. Yes! Looping is straightforward; it takes two teachers who believe in it and a principal who's willing to let them try it. It doesn't require numerous changes in curriculum, a huge outlay of money, or a lot of time to implement. It's about the easiest reform teachers will ever experience.

While there are ways to add complexity to the program in terms of instructional strategies that will optimize the looping arrangement (see pages 44, 51), the primary benefit from looping accrues from putting the same teacher into the same classroom with the same students for two years.

There are dangers in overstating the complexity and the benefits of looping. If it is presented as too complex, parents and school boards might steer away from a valuable school reform. If on the other hand the benefits are overstated, people will have unrealistic expectations, and the looping program, though in reality very successful, may be looked upon as a failure (see pages 18, 66, 78 and 91).

Q.

Looping seems to be widely accepted. Why do you think this is?

A.
1. It is a viable solution to the time-bound, 180-day school year.
2. It's a concept that many parents, whether they realize it or not, have requested. (How many teachers have heard parents say, "You've given Julie such a good year — I wish she could have you again next year!"?)
3. It is relatively easy and inexpensive to implement.
4. It works!

Looping is accepted primarily because it is based on one of the most basic human needs: the need to form strong, enduring relationships with others. When parents and teachers see the positive effects of the looping arrangement in the happy faces of the children, they are sold.

The acceptance of looping tends to snowball. Frequently by the middle of the second year parents not involved are requesting looping classrooms for their children, which leads to other teachers offering to create looping classrooms of their own.

Q.

Will looping boost standardized achievement scores?

A. It might — but that's not a good reason on which to base a decision to loop.

Ted Thibodeau, Assistant Superintendent of the Attleboro, Massachusetts, school district, the only wholly multi-year school district in the country, said in June of 1996 that "the standardized test scores did rise; the high scores stayed high, and the low scores came up." In a newspaper article in October of 1996, a sharp rise in Attleboro's test scores from the MEAP (Massachusetts Education Assessment Program) was reported. Thibodeau credited the two-year teacher assignments and reassignments of teachers, but also gave particular credit to the PALMS (Partnership to Advance Learning in Math and Science) program, as well as Attleboro's concentration on "better preparation in taking standardized tests."* He noted that it's also difficult to attribute a rise in test scores to a single factor, since most school systems implement a number of programs and instructional strategies at once that can impact on standardized test results.

The danger in presenting standardized test scores as a reason to loop is twofold: (1) it puts the emphasis on the wrong thing; and (2) there is a risk of putting a successful program in a bad light if the test scores do not go up.

Many of the important benefits of looping can't be measured on a standardized test; higher self-esteem, motivation to learn, more socially conscious behavior, and a sense of well-being are life-long benefits that can't be measured in stanines. The emphasis should not be on high test scores (even though that might occur), but on creating better lives for the children involved.

---

* Hand, Jim. "City test scores up sharply." *The Sun Chronicle*, October 22, 1996.

A. The same consistency and stability that benefit "regular" students also benefit children with special needs. In fact, special-needs students might require this predictable, supportive environment even more.

Some special-needs children have particular difficulties with acceptance; their normal need to belong is often thwarted by their handicaps. A looping classroom naturally seems to develop a close-knit, protective, familylike atmosphere where these handicaps or disabilities are taken in stride by the other students.

Of course, the extra instructional time, the long-term attention, and the observation and assessment by one adult over an extended period of time help as well. A teacher who has the opportunity to interact with a special-needs child over two years is going to have an enormous amount of insight into that child's strengths and weaknesses. Many multiyear teachers turn into very strong advocates for their "special" students.

Q.

Is the looping classroom a good placement for special-needs students?

Q.

How do late
readers fare
in a looping
classroom?

 A. They do very well, providing they receive appropriate instruction.

First-grade teachers in this country are under enormous pressure to make sure every child is reading by the end of first grade. Unfortunately, this is arbitrary and, for many children, unrealistic. Children learn to read anywhere from age five to age seven; this range is entirely normal. The problem is, when a first-grade teacher nears the end of the school year and some of her children still aren't reading, the school system looks upon the lack of reading skills as a failure.

The International Reading Association (IRA) has expressed concern that we are overidentifying late readers as needing special education services; we are helping to create this situation by drawing an arbitrary line in the sand for first graders.

The looping classroom erases that line in the sand. If a child is not reading fully by the end of first grade, the teacher can simply pick up where she left off at the beginning of second grade; most children will catch on by mid-fall of the second year.

Q.

Will children who are developmentally young "catch up" in a looping classroom?

A. Absolutely not — no more than they'd catch up in a straight single-grade class or a multiage classroom.

The reason is that they're not behind; they're right where they should be developmentally. In the past ten years, some experts have suggested that if children are in a developmentally appropriate setting, they will somehow magically catch up at grade three or grade four. One only needs to talk with elementary and middle grade teachers to realize the mythical nature of this conclusion.

It is important to understand that the looping classroom respects the developmental needs of students, but should not be considered a setting where children "catch up."

What Questions Do Most Parents Ask About Looping?

Q.

What if my child is placed with an ineffective teacher?

A. This is probably the greatest concern of parents, and it's a legitimate one. In her doctoral dissertation for the University of Sarasota, Elizabeth (Betty) Jankowski states, "Teachers are the most influential factor in the looping process."*

Many of us have had the experience of having a teacher who was either incompetent, ill-tempered, or both. It's a traumatic experience for a child even for one year; over two years, it can be harmful.

Jim Grant, when interviewed on *The Today Show* (March 9, 1996) said, "Some teachers shouldn't be with children one year, let alone two!" The reality is, however, that it is almost impossible these days for a school system to terminate an ineffective teacher's employment.

Fortunately, most looping situations at the present time are voluntary assignments, usually initiated by the teacher. Since marginal teachers don't usually put themselves on the cutting edge of change, there's a reduced chance that a student will be placed with an ineffectual teacher for two years in a row.

This will not necessarily alleviate parents' fears. The best way to prevent this from happening is to incorporate an "opt-out" clause into the looping program. At the end of the first year there needs to be a way for parents to politely and easily say that they want a different placement for their child for the next year.

In some school systems, other options are available. Attleboro, Massachusetts combines an "opt-out" policy (which few people take advantage of) with an energetic team teaching arrangement. Dr. Joseph Rappa, the superintendent of schools, sometimes assigns weak teachers with strong ones in order to bring up the weak teacher's ability level.

An ineffective teacher should not be given a two-year teaching assignment; this is within the power and scope of the school principal to prevent.

---

* Jankowski, Elizabeth. "Perceptions of the Effect of Looping on Classroom Relationships and Continuity of Learning." Doctoral dissertation. Hilton Head, SC, 1996.

Q.

What if there is a personality clash between the teacher and my child?

A. Actually the question is more likely to be, "What if that teacher seems to dislike my child?" The ultimate solution may be the same as in the previous question; that is, provide a year-end "opt-out" choice for the parents. But before this happens, the teacher and school administration should make every effort, for the child's sake, to resolve the conflict.

Sometimes, a conflict between a student and a teacher is the result of a misunderstanding, which can often be remedied; other times, the student's learning style may clash with the teacher's instructional style. Another example is a student who comes into the classroom with a hostile attitude that reflects the feelings of his or her parents.

In any case, an ongoing conflict between teacher and student can seriously damage the student's self-esteem and wear down the teacher, who often ends up feeling she can't do anything right.

At the base of many personality conflicts is a feeling of failure or lack of self-esteem on the part of the student. Yvette Zgonc, a nationally known educational consultant and lecturer on student behavior and discipline, suggests these methods of dealing with the issue:

1. First, ask yourself what you can do to help this kid succeed in class. Have you tried everything you can think of?
2. One of the best strategies is to conference with the kid, to talk about the problems he or she is having.
3. Talk to other colleagues who have had the child; what has worked for them?
4. Bring in the parents. Use the services of a guidance counselor, if possible, to help mediate the discussion.*

The teacher must be objective about the conflict and his or her role in it. If every avenue has been tried and the conflict is not resolved (and the student's self-esteem is seen to be suffering as a result), then the school, for the child's sake, should seek a different placement for the child.

---

* From *The Looping Handbook*, by Jim Grant, Bob Johnson and Irv Richardson. Peterborough, NH: Crystal Springs Books, 1996.

Q.

What if my child is placed in a difficult class for two years?

A. Every teacher has experienced a class that just never seems to click; that seems full of strong-willed, unruly children; or that is so overloaded with children with severe emotional needs that the quality of instruction and class atmosphere suffer.

If a group of children is this dysfunctional, it becomes a lose-lose situation; both students and teacher suffer, and the parents are bound to hear about the situation quickly and become concerned. This is a situation that requires intermediation.

• The first thing to do is analyze the classroom dynamics to see how each child contributes (in a positive or negative way) to the classroom atmosphere. Usually the teacher, who may initially feel that the entire class is dysfunctional, will realize that a few of the students are the main cause of the disorder. With the involvement and support of the administration, the guidance counselors, and the parents, the teacher needs to devise interventions for these children. Behavior contracts often work in these situations.

• If the interventions don't work, a team teaching arrangement might help manage a challenging classroom.

• If team teaching is not possible, or does not result in a positive, smooth-running classroom, then the administration should support reassigning some children. When placing children in a different classroom, be careful to present it as a positive move: "We're moving you to Mr. Smith's room so you'll have a chance to do more science." It's important to take the reason for the move off the child to avoid hurt feelings.

Q.

If two years with the same teacher is good, why not keep them three, or four, or more?

A. We feel that most children stand to benefit enormously from two years with the same teacher, and could probably benefit from three; but more than that has potential drawbacks.

First, the parent support is very strong for a two-year teacher-student relationship, but drops off at three years. Many parents and educators feel that children benefit from exposure to the talents and the viewpoints of a variety of teachers during the course of their education. They are also concerned that their children may miss out on new friendships if they're kept with the same group of students indefinitely.

Another concern is that the teacher's strengths are magnified — but so are his or her weaknesses. We must be careful not to turn a teacher weakness into a student weakness.

Of course, opinions differ. The Waldorf schools, which have been operating since the turn of the century, assign a group of students to one teacher who stays with those students from first through the eighth grades. The depth of love and understanding that develops between teacher and child in this type of long-term relationship can be profound. It is an option that some parents choose for their children; but this arrangement would probably not work in most of today's public schools.

Q.

My child is gifted. Will her abilities be challenged if she has the same teacher for two years?

A. This is a valid concern, not just for the parents of gifted children, but for all parents.

The looping classroom is ideal for providing enrichment activities. Since the teacher can develop a curriculum plan over a two-year period, he doesn't have to worry about "stepping on the toes" of the teacher in the next grade, at least in the middle of the two-year span. He can accelerate students in the first year, and extend the teaching horizontally in the second year.

The looping classroom is also conducive to implementing the type of independent learning strategies — learning centers, independent research, and team-based projects — that allow children to seek their own depth and direct their own learning.

The best way to deal with this question is to share your two-year curriculum plan with parents. This will show what you plan to teach and how the learning can either be accelerated or enriched by allowing the child to dig deeper into the areas of study.

Gifted Children in a Two-Year Classroom

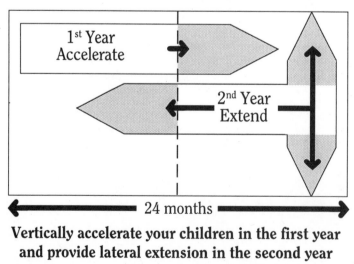

1st Year Accelerate

2nd Year Extend

← 24 months →

Vertically accelerate your children in the first year and provide lateral extension in the second year

Q. Two of my children are in the same class. How will a looping classroom affect this?

A. Many parents share concerns about a child being in the same class as a sibling, and the concern deepens when the siblings face two years together in a looping classroom.

It is important to realize that siblings are individuals and should be treated as such. Teachers need to avoid drawing comparisons between the two children and should give them opportunities to work both together as classmates, and separately with other classmates. Making sure siblings separate and work with others allows each child to develop socially in his or her own way, and avoids the prospect of one sibling becoming dominant and making educational and social decisions for the other child — at least during class time.

Most teachers who have considered this question have found the situation not to be a problem in the classroom; but it is a valid concern which needs to be addressed with parents as it arises.

Q.

Here we go again. Isn't looping just the latest fad in education?

A. Looping is not new; the U.S. Department of the Interior referred to the benefits of teacher rotation as early as 1913. The concept is becoming increasingly popular around the United States, and is referred to by many names:

- multiyear teaching
- teach for two
- take 'em up
- roll 'em over
- teacher retention
- teacher rotation
- 20 month classroom
- two-cycle teaching
- step-up
- teacher-student progression.

It's not a fad, either. For almost a century, Waldorf schools have been keeping students together with the same teacher from first through eighth grade. Looping has also been practiced for many years in Germany, Scandinavia, Japan, and Israel.

Looping has grown out of the natural desire of teachers and parents, who recognize the importance of long-term relationships in children's lives, to do the best they can for their children.

Most fads start with a lot of fanfare and vanish as soon as the next one comes down the pike. Real reform starts small, makes sense, and builds as people see positive results.

A. The best way to respond to this question is to make sure that you and your administration delineate the reasons you have chosen to implement looping. Then develop a way to monitor the expected gains, whether they be improved attendance, fewer discipline problems, improved performance, or another anticipated benefit.

The Attleboro, Massachusetts, school system has armed itself with some solid statistics to prove its case for multiyear teaching assignments:

Q.

How will I know if looping is working better than single-year classrooms?

Student attendance in grades 2 through 8 has been increased from 92 percent average daily attendance (ADA) to 97.2 percent ADA. Retention rates have decreased by over 43 percent in those same grades. Discipline and suspensions, especially at the middle schools (grades 5 through 8), have declined significantly. Special education referrals have decreased by over 55 percent, and staff attendance has improved markedly from an average of seven days absent per staff member per year, to less than three.*

---

* Rappa, Joseph B. "Presentation to the National Education Commission on Time and Learning," Cambridge, MA, September 24, 1993. Quoted in *The Looping Handbook*, p. 15.

Q.

Will my child have a more difficult time saying goodbye to his teacher after two years?

 A. It is true that saying goodbye to close relationships that exist between teacher and child and even among classmates is difficult. Teachers report that it is difficult to say goodbye to the parents, too.

Even though anxiety about the end of a two-year looping classroom is a valid concern, and separation does seem more stressful compared to a single-grade, single-year classroom, we feel that the solid emotional foundation that two years in a looping classroom provides more than makes up for that.

Sometimes teachers and parents worry about separation anxiety unnecessarily. One Rhode Island teacher reported that she had a boy who experienced difficulties with transitions; she and the boy's parents were very worried once it came time for him to leave his two-year classroom and move on. It turned out the boy was looking forward to the change, and to making new friends. Apparently the two years with this teacher and this class had given him an emotional foundation that made him ready to step out into the world.*

Separation anxiety can be minimized with a little planning. Here are some suggestions:

- Take your students to visit the next grade level and meet the teacher they will have next year.

- Give your students an opportunity to interview children from the next grade level to find out what to expect.

- Share highlights of the curriculum for the next year. (*Don't* tell your students scary stories about how hard it will be!)

- Give the parents a chance to visit the next grade level and meet the new teacher. This is especially important if the children are moving on to a new building as well as a different grade.

_____
* From *The Looping Handbook*, p. 114.

- Plan a reunion with your former students sometime in the fall; this will give your students a sense that even though your time as their teacher has ended, your caring relationship hasn't.

Finally, let your parents know that you understand their concerns and will do whatever you can to ease their children's transition.

Q.

What if my child moves from a looping classroom to a single-year classroom?

A. The evidence from teachers and parents seems to be that children who have the experience of a positive two-year classroom do very well in a single-grade class, and seem to retain the gains made in the looping class — they fit in well with their new classmates, retain their ability to direct their own learning, are usually very solid academically, have a better attitude toward school, and show sensitivity to others, making them positive role models for their classmates.

The downside seems to be that if students have a looping teacher who gives them the reins in terms of directing their own learning and having ownership in the classroom, it can be a difficult transition to have a teacher who exerts more control over the learning process. This is more a matter of adapting to differing teaching styles than a looping issue. It may be more likely to happen with looping or multiage, because teachers in these settings tend to encourage students to take an active role in their learning.

Q.

Is it important to have a choice about sending my child to a looping classroom or to a regular classroom?

A. We feel that, when possible, parents should have a choice in this issue.

Parents have expressed a number of reasons for not wanting their child to loop. Some parents:

- only understand a conventional single-year, single-grade classroom.
- may be opposed to their child having a particular teacher for a two-year period.
- may want their child to be with a teacher of a certain gender; many single mothers, for instance, request that their child be placed with a male teacher to give their child a positive male role model.
- want to take a "wait and see" attitude, especially if looping is a new concept in their child's school.

Whatever the reason for parents' resistance, giving them choices whenever you can goes a long way toward gaining their trust and their support when you need them in your corner.

Q.

Are there some children who might not do well in a multi-year classroom?

 A. Yes; but for the most part this has more to do with the child's reaction to the specific situation than the concept of looping. Some children:

- come into the classroom jaded because of parental attitudes.
- do not fit in with the other classmates.
- have a learning style incompatible with the teacher's instructional style.
- develop a personality conflict with the teacher.

These children may need a fresh start in a new classroom in order to get back on track.

Also, some children simply like change; they look forward to having a new teacher and meeting new friends each year, and may feel confined by the looping arrangement.

No one educational structure is right for every child; the best advice for school systems is to create choices whenever possible, to allow for different needs of students, parents, and teachers.

Q.

Is there research available on looping?

A. Most of the research available is based on anecdotal records in the form of questionnaires and surveys. Several studies have been conducted on multiyear programs, with overwhelmingly positive results, particularly in the affective areas.

• The **National Middle Schools Association** has published a study of the Lincoln Middle School of Gainesville, Florida; an excerpt from this study is available in *The Multiage Handbook*; to receive a copy of the entire study, contact:

> The National Middle Schools Association
> 2600 Corp. Exchange Drive
> Suite 370
> Columbus, OH 43231

This study reports higher achievement levels among middle school students, much lower rates of discipline problems, and, what is of particular importance, an overwhelming increase in positive attitudes among staff, indicating a much higher willingness to work with and mentor students.

• The **Attleboro, Massachusetts**, school district has conducted statistical studies showing many positive results of multiyear teacher assignments (see page 31), as well as parent and teacher surveys showing a high approval rating from both groups. The Attleboro School District is covered in *The Looping Handbook*, which contains interviews with assistant superintendent Theodore (Ted) Thibodeau, as well as several teachers and administrators from four different schools in the district.

Anyone wishing to contact the district directly, either for more statistical information or to arrange for a visit to the district, should contact:

> Ted Thibodeau
> Attleboro School District
> 100 Rathbun Williard Drive
> Attleboro, MA 02703-2798

• Elizabeth Jankowski, Ed.D., wrote her doctoral dissertation for the University of Sarasota, Florida, on "The Perception of the Effect of Looping on Classroom Relationships and Continuity in Learning." Jankowski, a counselor at Hilton Head Elementary School in Hilton Head, South Carolina, reported positive attitudes among parents and students and positive effects on instructional progress, volunteerism among parents, and cooperation among students. Results were measured by parent, student, and teacher surveys and by the use of the BASC Self Report of Personality C test.

To contact Jankowski about her research write:

Elizabeth Jankowski, Ed.D.
Hilton Head Elementary School
10 Wilborn Road
Hilton Head, SC 29926

A. Multiage is a powerful, positive instructional strategy, and it does have a few advantages not present in a looping setting. For example, when children of different ages work together in a multiage class, the younger children learn from the older ones, and the older children have the opportunity to be positive role models for the younger ones.

However, multiage is more complex than looping. It takes longer to implement, requires more research and planning (and therefore more in the way of start-up money), and involves teaching curriculum standards to more than one grade level at a time.

Many communities have grade-specific content standards and grade-level standardized testing that can make it difficult to create the truly seamless, continuous progress curriculum that is a major goal of multiage education.

Some communities are also very conservative and might look upon multiage education as unacceptable, but find looping more palatable.

Q. I've heard a lot about multiage; now it's looping. When and why is looping more advisable than multiage?

How Will Looping Affect Me as a Teacher?

Q.

If I decide to loop, will it require extra work?

A. At the beginning, it involves extra time and effort, but you'll enjoy it. In the long run, we think you'll save more time than you've spent preparing to loop.

The first thing you'll need to do is familiarize yourself with your school's curriculum requirements for both grade levels that you'll be teaching (see page 52 for ideas on how to blend the curriculum).

You'll need to understand the developmental stages for children at both grade levels. You may have to learn a specialized curriculum (various states require grade-specific instruction in certain areas like health and drug education). You may move to a grade that requires standardized testing. You may want or need to move to a different room, or to rearrange your room to adapt it to the next grade level.

All this extra work pays off, however, on that 181st day of school, when your students come into your room after summer vacation, and within ten minutes are in the swing of the new year.

A. No. First, it is important to believe that it will work! It is one education reform grounded in common sense.

Teachers change grade levels for a number of reasons in their careers. Many move to the next level because of numbers or seniority issues, and end up teaching the same class of students for two years. Other teachers request a change in grade level. This natural fluctuation in staffing assignments within a school can be used to introduce looping into a school.

Looping can be initiated by a principal, who in most school districts has the power to reassign teachers within her school, saying, "How would you like to move from first grade to second? And by the way, how about taking your students with you?" It can be that simple and that quiet.

Q.

If I try looping and it doesn't work, am I going to lose my job?

Q.

Will I need special training to teach in a two-year classroom?

A. There are certain instructional strategies — thematic learning, cooperative learning, learning centers, conflict resolution, cooperative discipline practices — that will optimize the looping experience for your students, but these are good teaching practices for any classroom.

One important component of a looping teacher's training is an understanding of the developmental range of the children she will be teaching over the two-year span. An excellent book on children's stages of development is *Yardsticks: Children in the Classroom Ages 4–14*, by Chip Wood.

Consider doing a personal needs assessment to decide what you will need to pursue in your looping classroom. You should look at your potential needs in terms of:

- instructional strategies
- management
- materials
- space
- support

We recommend you not try to change too many things at once. Choose an area that is already a strength and build on that. As you become comfortable with new teaching strategies, then decide on your next step.

When you consider learning new strategies, visit classrooms where positive techniques are being used. Attend seminars. Read magazines, journals, and books.

Build on your present foundation, though, and be careful not to overwhelm yourself with too much at once.

A. A good multiyear teacher should:

- want to teach children for more than one year.
- think developmentally about students.
- have experience teaching different grade levels.
- be able to manage risk.
- be open to change.
- be prepared for hard work and long hours.
- enjoy challenging the status quo.
- have experience in effective classroom instructional and management techniques.
- avoid adopting every new fad that comes along.
- respect developmental diversity.
- enjoy collaborating with teaching colleagues.
- have high energy and common sense.

The most important quality of a multiyear teacher should be a love of children.

Q.

What qualities are desirable in a multiyear teacher?

Q.

What will it be like having the same parents over two years?

A. Most teachers find that by the second year they have solid backing from their parent group; parents are glad to see their children in a strong reliable relationship with the teacher, and see themselves as partners with the teacher in doing what's right for their children. The teacher and parents end up monitoring the children and planning how to meet the children's needs together.

Parents of children in a multiyear setting tend to become more actively involved during the second year, donating both time and materials to the classroom. This parental involvement ends up having a profoundly positive effect on the children. Dave and Jan Ulrey, educational consultants on multiage practices, have noted that children of involved parents:

- do better academically.
- get along better with their parents.
- participate in more activities with their parents.
- have a more positive attitude about school.

As for parents who become more active, they are more likely to:

- feel more confident about school for their children.
- have positive feelings about the school and school personnel.
- be more willing to work for the school.
- be able to help their children do better in school.

In the case of a child who is having difficulties in school — who is a late reader, for instance — the two-year span of the multiyear class can help calm down parents who are concerned about their child's success; the teacher and parents can work together, calmly, over a longer period to plan instructional strategies and home/school activities that will help get the child on track. The removal of that first-year deadline in June is undoubtedly very reassuring to parents whose child has experienced a bumpy start.

A. This can happen. That is why, when setting up the parameters of your looping classroom with your looping partner and your principal, you should establish predetermined guidelines about what will happen should this occur.

Many times it's possible to work out differences between teachers and parents. Obviously, this is the most desirable solution. If the enmity between a teacher and a set of parents is so obvious that it's becoming painful for the child caught in the middle, or if the parents are so difficult that it is seriously compromising the teacher's ability to do his job in a balanced way, then something has to be done.

Q. What if I have some especially difficult parents for two years in a row?

One way to avoid this situation is to provide the parents with an "opt-out" clause that allows them to request another placement for their child after the end of the first year of the multiyear assignment. If the parents have a lot of hostility toward the teacher, it is hoped that they will accept the chance to say goodbye and move on to another teacher.

Most schools that loop and that have an opt-out clause find that the parents rarely use it. If a teacher has a set of extremely difficult parents, and the parents don't volunteer to opt out, the administration should encourage the option in a meeting, and try to find a way to turn the proposed move into a positive one. ("Mr. Casey is good at challenging active boys like Johnny, Mr. Firestarter!")

If for some reason the parents are against the move, then it is up to the principal to make a decision. We encourage the administration to back the teacher, and not allow him to be subjected to oppositional parents for a period as long as two years.

Q.

How does looping affect teachers' attitudes about their jobs?

A. It must help quite a bit, because they show up for work more often. The multiyear school district of Attleboro, Massachusetts discovered that their average staff absentee rate of seven days per year dropped below three days per year once they instituted multiyear assignments.

Looping teachers enjoy going to school, largely because the two-year arrangement lessens the pressure of all the requirements they face. Without lowering academic standards, they can take time to assess and address children's differing needs, plan for in-depth teaching of the curriculum, and assess, plan, and monitor interventions.

Even though looping can involve more work initially (see page 42), it ends up being much less emotionally taxing, because essentially a looping teacher has twice as much time to get to know students and parents. The relationships formed are likely to be deeper and more supportive on all sides.

You might think of the teacher in a single-year, single-grade classroom as a sprinter, who, heart pounding, adrenaline pumping, has to pour on all the energy and speed at her command to reach the June finish line. The looping teacher, on the other hand, is like the long-distance runner — she finds her pace, gets into a groove, and just keeps moving.

Q. Would team teaching be a good arrangement in a looping classroom?

A. Yes, it can be extremely effective. As a matter of fact, several parental concerns can be put to rest by creating a good teaching team.

Parents might be concerned that their child is placed with a teacher for two years in a row who isn't particularly strong in a certain subject (math, for example). With a team arrangement, a savvy principal can put together two individuals with different academic strengths, so that one team member teaches reading, writing, and social studies, for instance, while the other member teaches math and science. Teachers can also cooperatively teach some subjects and take turns assisting in other subjects.

Devising large group, small group and individualized instruction is much easier and more efficient with two teachers in the room. Some schools have even hired one teacher certified in special education as a member of a two-member team, or have included a special education teacher as a third member of a team. These teaming structures have been very successful at integrating special-needs students into the regular classroom without shortchanging other students.

Another concern, both of parents and teachers, is when a personality conflict develops between a teacher and a child. A good teaching team can short-circuit that; while one teacher may have a difficult time with a particular child, the other team member may not. Their instructional strategies and personal approach may be more compatible with the child's needs, which can help ameliorate any potential problems. The same theory can also work in a parent-teacher personality conflict.

The recently published book, *Team Teaching,** lists a number of benefits to students of team teaching:

- The student receives more individual attention; there is more time to tune in to individual student needs.
- Children in need of special support can be pulled aside in small groups and helped.
- Students are never left unattended.
- Interaction with students increases.

---

* Northern Nevada Writing Project Teacher-Researcher Group. *Team Teaching.* York, ME: Stenhouse Publishers, 1997.

- A teacher is always on hand to help with a thought or a spelling word, or to explain what is expected in the lesson.
- Someone is always available to walk around and monitor learning.
- Someone is available to answer questions.
- The curriculum moves on even if one teacher is absent.
- There is a better chance of finding out whether there is a breakdown in communication.
- Thought processes can be modeled.
- There is flexibility in paperwork and assignments.
- Students are given less busywork.
- Students can be helped to look for alternatives.
- There is more time to introduce more detailed information.
- There are more opportunities to read.
- Students learn how to ask questions.
- Students are exposed to more ideas.
- Students can relate to more than one teacher personally.
- Teachers can use different skills in different situations.
- Discipline is easier. The partners have the ability to consult with each other and to plan strategy.
- Students can be assessed informally by one teacher while the other leads the class.
- Grading and evaluation are enhanced because there are two views of the student.
- A student's social, emotional, and curricular needs can be discussed with another person who has an equal understanding of the child.
- Situations that develop without warning can be given immediate attention.
- Students can observe a good working relationship between adults and experience a positive role model for adult interaction.
- There is more flexibility to make phone calls to parents.
- Conferences are easier, and the parents get more than one view of the child.

Teaching teams are formed for a variety of reasons, some philosophical, others demographic or financial. Some teachers have a choice in the process; others are informed that they'll be doing this, and might be assigned a team member.

Whatever the reasons a teaching team is formed, the structure requires hard work, open communication, negotiating ability, and emotional maturity on the part of both team members for the arrangement to succeed. Teaming isn't for everyone. Ideally, the administration should incorporate an "opt-out" clause into the implementation plan.

A. Yes, there are strategies you can use to make learning more effective in a multiyear classroom. Thematic planning, simulations, cooperative grouping, and strategies to help children become independent learners are all particularly suitable for the multiyear classroom. Learning centers are a valuable tool here; if you don't have a lot of space for learning centers, you can create megacenters, turning your classroom into a resource area where students take on more responsibility for locating and choosing materials that provide practice, enrichment, or extension for their learning.

Since a looping classroom is such a positive social experience for children, you might also want to explore acceptance activities (to deal with issues of special-needs kids) and themes that develop an understanding of social and cultural diversity. Conflict resolution is an effective technique that encourages self-management and responsibility for one's own behavior, rather than having the students rely on a teacher to "control" the group.

The continuity provided in a looping classroom can be enhanced by creating a "summer bridge" of activities for children at the end of the first year (see page 56).

Q. Are there any teaching strategies that are particularly effective in a looping classroom?

Q.

How can I blend my curriculum to make it more effective and meaningful over two years?

A. Looping provides a great opportunity to integrate your curriculum and provide meaningful, enjoyable learning experiences for your children over a two-year span, as opposed to just *covering* material in isolated bits across one school year.

A good way to start is to create a chart or a graphic organizer listing all the academic areas you will teach. Next, add the different concepts and skills that you want to teach, including any topics such as multiple intelligences and real-world connections you want to emphasize. Then, pull together:

1. any curriculum requirements from your district.
2. any state testing requirements.
3. any national testing requirements.
4. any child-driven interests, projects, and themes that your students would like to pursue.
5. any interests of your own that you would like to pursue with your students.

Dovetail all these pieces and plan your curriculum over your two-year instructional period, integrating the instruction whenever possible, making sure you plan activities for whole group, small group, and individual learning.

A. Schools are moving in the direction of using authentic, ongoing assessment tools to monitor "how we are doing" instead of "how did we do?" With looping, you have time to take better advantage of these tools. For instance:

- anecdotal notes become very important to help you make crucial decisions regarding children.
- portfolios or folders with student work help you to gauge their progress.
- rubrics are good tools to assess where children are before instruction, and to gauge their progress after instruction has taken place. Rubrics also help you, as a teacher, plan and assess your own instruction.
- projects based on multiple intelligences and connected to thematic units allow children to demonstrate what they've learned in ways other than pencil-and-paper methods.

There is a danger in a looping classroom that potential learning problems might be overlooked because of the forgiving nature of the classroom (see pages 69-70); therefore, it is doubly important to have a good reliable method of ongoing, authentic assessment in place.

Q.

How do I assess students in a looping classroom?

Q.

If I decide to loop, should I stay in the same room for two years, or should I move to a new room for the second year?

A. The decision concerning this frequently asked question is best left to the teachers involved. Some actually move their classrooms to accommodate parents who want their children to feel promoted to another classroom for the second year. Other teachers choose to stay in the same room, primarily because they have so much "stuff" that it would be a hardship to move.

Usually, teachers who remain in the same classroom are careful to change key components in the room. In fact, at the end of the first year, we suggest that looping teachers involve their students in May or June, by asking them to design what they would like their classroom to look like the second year. This typical "down" time in June can be put to good use by empowering students to prepare next year's folders, portfolios, journals, reading logs, classroom environment, etc.

When deciding how to handle classroom space assignments, it is important to remember that each school has its own individual circumstances to consider. Here are some thoughts for both options:

Reasons to Consider Remaining in the Same Classroom

- You will be using most of your own materials that it would be a true hardship to move.
- There is no strong reason for moving and it would use up valuable energy and time.
- The physical space is appropriate for your teaching style.
- If only a few teachers are looping, you might prefer to stay in your own classroom if it does not greatly affect the dynamics of your class in relation to the rest of the school. For example, if you teach third grade, then loop to fourth, will it matter if students remain in your classroom, while other third graders move to another area of the building for fourth grade? In some schools this is a concern, while in others it is not.

Reasons to Consider Changing Classrooms

- If you have a kindergarten/first grade loop, it is advisable to ensure that kindergartners be in a physical space that is developmentally appropriate for their needs.

- You and your partner are comfortable sharing the bulk of the materials. The materials can remain and the teachers move, particularly when classrooms are assigned in groups according to grade level.

- If only a few teachers are looping in a school with designated grade-level wings, you might choose to move if it is important for students to be with their peers. You might also want to be with other teachers at your grade level; there are times when teachers feel left out of grade level decisions and activities when they are in a different physical space.

Q.

Are there ways I can use the summer months after the first year to get a head start on the second year?

A. Yes. Actually, as educators become involved in looping, they are discovering that a summer "bridge," linking the first and second year of a looping classroom, is a very important part of the practice. Many teachers assign reading, summer projects, correspondence, and even parent/child activities that help children maintain their skills over the summer months.

Some schools plan organized summer activities at the school, as well as summer field trips, to keep the children's education on a roll through the summer, and to keep the family atmosphere of the looping classroom alive.*

With the summer bridge added to an already flexible two-year curriculum, a looping classroom can actually approach the ideal of a two-year, continuous progress configuration.

---

* See *The Looping Handbook* for summer activities contributed by teachers from three different schools. (Portions of the activities included in the handbook were excerpted from *The Multiyear Lesson Plan Book* by Char Forsten.)

Q. What if I have a student who can't adjust no matter what I seem to do?

A. Children can be a handful in an infinite number of ways; they can be hostile, extremely active, polite but oppositional, uncooperative, emotionally unstable — the list is endless. One year with such a child is draining; many teachers are worried that two years would be overwhelming.

This is a tricky subject, because many times the children who make the most demands on a teacher are the very children who could benefit the most from a two-year classroom. Certainly a number of strategies should be tried in the first year to ameliorate the child's negative behavior. Student ownership in class rules and classroom structure, conflict resolution, behavior contracts, cooperative discipline, acceptance activities, and other things can be tried to effect a positive change.

The teacher must also look behind the child's behavior to the cause of the problem. Why is the child acting out? Maybe some extension or enrichment activities are needed. Does the child have a hidden learning disability, or other difficulties learning the required materials? He or she may need diagnostic tests, tutoring, and possibly special education interventions to deal with learning problems.

It may also be as simple as teacher and child not being a good match for one another, and ending up in a personality clash. (For more about personality clashes, see page 25.) In this case, after *all* other interventions have been tried, if the situation doesn't clear up, it makes sense for the teacher and the administration to consider moving the child to a better placement, either at the end of the first year, or in some cases, mid-year.

Q.

Should a teacher be assigned to a looping classroom against her will?

A. *No!* The best way to make sure that a new educational reform does not work is to mandate it. Teachers have had this happen to them, and most of them adapt, but some do not; and they are the ones who can sink a new reform.

The teachers who volunteer for a concept like looping are exactly the ones an administration should want to spearhead a reform. Usually the volunteers are high-energy, committed, conscientious people who will do anything to make life better for their students; and they will do the groundbreaking work. Usually once they succeed, a few more teachers will dip their toes into the water; then more will follow. But there will always be teachers who, for one reason or another, want to stay at one grade-level.

We recommend a school provide options for parents: both looping classrooms and single-year, single-grade classrooms at each grade level (plus multiage groupings, if appropriate). Those teachers who do not want to loop can be made to feel that they are making an important contribution to parental choice, which is a vital part of the success of any school.

Q.

Every time my school adopts a new reform, there is staff dissension. How can we avoid that with looping?

A. Staff dissension is a big issue with any reform, and looping is no exception. There are always ways to avoid or minimize the problem, however.

Here are some suggestions to avoid unnecessary friction among staff while starting up your new program:

- Even though a few teachers may choose to loop, involve all staff members in the process.

- Attitude is everything. Create a positive, safe atmosphere for all staff members.

- Build in a communications component for the first five to ten minutes of your faculty meetings, and use it to update the staff on looping's progress. Allow an open question-and-answer period during this time.

- Be careful not to create an elitist program by placing all of the school's gifted students in the looping program.

- Nothing splits a staff more quickly than unequal class size. Make sure your looping classroom has the same class size as other classrooms at the same grade level. (At the same time, be protective of your own class in terms of size. You shouldn't be required to carry more than your share of students.)

- Place the same number of special-needs students in your multiyear program as any other classroom at the same grade level — not fewer, and definitely not more.

- When students transfer out of your classroom be sure to take your turn receiving new students.

- Giving your classroom a regal-sounding name, i.e., *The Wonder Years* or *The Platinum Program,* will almost always give fellow staff members the feeling that you think your program is somehow superior to theirs.

- Publicly comparing the benefits of being in your two-year program versus being placed in a 36-week classroom always divides the staff. Always represent your program as one of several fine options at your school.

- Plan, assess, then revise. Don't try to avoid problems. This tends to push them underground, where energy is used to suppress feelings instead of being applied to the complex role of teaching students.

- Remember that if a teacher expresses hesitancy with looping *now*, it doesn't necessarily mean he or she doesn't want to loop *ever*. Especially in the beginning of a new reform, there may be some teachers with ill health, or with responsibilities at home such as caring for an ailing parent, that may make it difficult to contribute all the energy necessary to get the new practice started. Let the enthusiastic volunteers begin the program, and give other teachers the option of waiting for a more appropriate time to join in the reform.

A. Yes. As the teacher, you are the pivot around which looping revolves, and the administration should listen to you as you express your needs and desires. As a teacher, you should be able to:

- decide between teaching a single-grade, single-year classroom and a looping classroom.
- have a say in transferring a difficult student out of the classroom after the first year of a looping class.
- limit the number of high-needs children you will have over the two-year period.
- have a say in keeping a child for two years whose parents are difficult.
- create a balanced, teachable student population.
- move a child out of the multiyear program mid-year should the child and parents become dissatisfied with the program.
- be an integral part of an ongoing assessment process.

Q.

Should I, as a teacher, have a strong say in this reform?

All of the above issues should be negotiated with the administration before looping goes into effect, and parameters need to be created and communicated with staff and parents before the program's inception.

Of course, it's not always possible to have a choice in all of these matters. Some school districts have high concentrations of high-needs students; others have schools who may have only one classroom for each grade-level, in which case transferring a child is impossible. But you, as a teacher, need to give as much input as you can.

Q.

Are there some hidden consequences I should consider before deciding to loop?

A. Yes. There are some hidden consequences involved in a decision to loop that you need to be aware of:

- You might lose your teaching assistant if you move up a grade.
- You're going to have to learn a new curriculum at a different grade level.
- You might need to learn a specialized curriculum for a particular grade level (many states mandate drug education or health education in specific grades, for instance).
- You might run into grade-specific promotional standards.
- You might run into grade-specific standardized testing.
- You may lose close friends among your colleagues if you have to loop out of your pod.
- You may be moving to a very high-pressure grade, such as grade one or three.
- You may move to a grade level that is philosophically different than the grade level you're currently in.
- You may move to a grade level that requires an increase in class size.
- Some states may require you to hold two teacher certifications.
- You may be a member of a union that requires posting of a "new job opening" before a teacher may change to a different grade level. This effectively destroys the concept of looping, since a teacher has to compete with other teachers before moving to the next grade.

This All Sounds Too Good To Be True! Are There Downsides With Looping?

Q.

What are the obstacles to creating a looping classroom?

A. Probably the biggest obstacle is the perception of looping by teachers unfamiliar with the concept:

- Lack of customized planning seems to be an issue. There is no one recipe for looping that schools can adopt. Creating a flexible plan with a transitional time period to implement looping should be the first step in the process. Ongoing assessment and dialogues are critical to successful change.

- Sometimes teachers feel that parents won't like the concept, and see that as an obstacle. Many teachers hesitant to propose looping are surprised to learn that most parents readily support the idea.

- Some teachers work in an unsupportive environment, and hesitate to go out on a limb by trying something new and different.

- Some teachers feel that support from the school principal or other administration members is lacking, and that if they run into difficulty, they will not be helped by their superiors.

- A teacher waiting to loop may not find a teacher at the previous or next grade level willing to try the concept.

- A particular class of students may not represent a balanced population.

Once the looping class has begun, the administration should continue to monitor the process for possible personality conflicts within the classroom, shifts in class needs that create balance issues, and possible staff dissension.

Q.

Is there a danger that a multiyear classroom will become a dumping ground for high-needs students?

A. Yes, and it tends to be due to the success of multiyear classrooms. Principals have figured out that children with handicaps are better off with one teacher for multiple years, whether it's in a single-grade looping classroom or in a multiage classroom, and tend to overstock these classrooms with high-needs, high-maintenance kids.

Also, teachers in these classrooms tend to be the staff members with broad shoulders who can be persuaded to take on "just one more." The problem is that with too high a proportion of special-needs kids, the class soon becomes unmanageable, and the benefits of looping are lost as the teacher struggles to meet everyone's needs. The positive role modeling offered by regular education students is diminished as well. Children without special needs are often neglected and find their own basic needs unmet.

By all means, include special-needs students in looping classrooms; the best way to do this is to create an equitable placement plan for the entire school. If there are too many special-needs kids for the number of looping classes available, either create more looping classrooms or insist on a very careful placement process for these kids. Don't forget, in most schools there are single-grade teachers with lots of love and broad shoulders, too.

Q.

Are looping classrooms ever created for the wrong reasons?

 Yes; and the danger is that you may end up with a successful program being deemed a failure, because it is being judged by unrealistic expectations.

Here are some wrong reasons to start a looping program:

- to save money. It might save a little; it might even bring in a little, if your funding is based on average daily attendance and your attendance improves; but it is not a big money saver.

- to boost test scores. Test scores may or may not go up. Even if they do, there are usually too many variables to be able to accurately tie the rise in scores solely to looping.

- because it's a "cutting edge" reform. Don't base your rationale for adopting educational concepts on their being the "latest thing"; there's another one coming along in about six months. If you earn a reputation as someone who jumps on every bandwagon that comes along, you'll lose your credibility with your parents, who are your closest allies.

- to eliminate transition grades. Transition grades are created primarily to give extra time to children who are developmentally young. Looping, while a great educational practice, won't cause children to develop faster than their normal, built-in rate.

- to replace special education services. While looping is a great way to support children with special needs, it does not replace other, specific interventions for children with learning disabilities, slow learners, or children with physical disabilities that impact learning. A school district that tries to save money by replacing needed special ed services with regular looping classrooms, without supporting those classrooms with special ed staff, is courting disaster — and risking lawsuits.

Remember – the teacher is at the heart of a successful looping classroom and students are the focus. Any reasons for adopting looping should be tied to that fact.

A. Yes; there are instances where this is advisable. The teacher, administration and parents should look at the possibility of another placement for the child if:

- a teacher's instructional style cannot be reconciled with the student's learning style.

- the student and her parents have a negative attitude toward the teacher that can't be resolved.

- a child has special needs that can be better addressed by another teacher.

- the child simply cannot adjust to the teacher and his classmates.

Of course, all efforts should first be made to resolve whatever difficulties are preventing the child from fitting in; and any alternative placement should be one that is in the best interests of the child, and not merely a way to remove a student from a particular class.

Q.

Are there valid reasons to transfer a student from a looping classroom to a single-year classroom?

Q.

Is there a danger of a particular child becoming a 'teacher's pet'?

A. The 'teacher's pet' syndrome is a danger in any classroom; teachers naturally will relate to some children better than others, and will respond more spontaneously to some children than to others. In a two-year situation, this can become much more of a danger.

A major benefit of looping is the close relationship that can form between teacher and child; but if one child becomes a teacher's pet, the results can be harmful in many ways:

- The other students can become aware of the situation, and reject the 'teacher's pet', causing a sense of isolation in the favored student.

- The students may feel neglected in favor of the 'pet', which has a negative impact on their self-esteem.

- The teacher may in fact *be* neglecting other students, offering enrichment opportunities and individual attention that should be spread around the classroom.

- Disproportionate attention paid to one student at the expense of others can put an enormous amount of emotional pressure on the chosen student and create a distorted view of self that is very hard to reconcile.

Q. Is there a danger of overlooking a student's potential learning disability in a multiyear classroom?

A. Yes, the problem is very real. Because the looping classroom deemphasizes the graded barrier at the end of the first year, there is not the pressure to make high-stakes decisions such as retention and special education referrals. This is actually beneficial; children are less likely to be "over-referred" to special ed.

There is such a thing as a "halo effect," however, where the teacher and child develop such a close relationship that the teacher becomes too forgiving of a child's shortcomings.

It is doubly important in a two-year classroom for a teacher to provide on-going, authentic assessment for children in order to stay on top of their skills levels, strengths and weaknesses. It is also the teacher's responsibility to gauge whether a child's lagging abilities will be resolved by a little extra time and instructional modifications, or whether the problems exhibited by the child represent a potential learning disability.

Gretchen Goodman, a national education consultant and author of *Inclusive Classrooms From A to Z* and *I Can Learn! Strategies and Activities for Gray-Area Children*, offers the following guide to gauging a child's potential need for special services:

A child with a possible learning disability may show some of the following signs:

- Has difficulty retaining knowledge taught.
- Requires a number of repetitions of taught materials (rate of acquisition and knowledge retention are lower than those of age-appropriate peers).
- Lacks organizational strategies to work independently.
- Is unable to discriminate between important facts and details and unnecessary facts.
- Is unable to remain attentive and focused on learning — inability to focus does affect the learning continuum.
- Experiences difficulties with expressive and receptive language.
- Often lacks motivation.

- Exhibits inappropriate social skills.
- Experiences difficulty memorizing and applying new information.
- Requires work load and time allowances to be adapted to specific need.
- May display poor judgment calls.
- May be unable to transition from one activity to another.
- May learn best when taught through a multisensory approach.*

A teacher who suspects a learning disability should refer the child for evaluation. If the results show a disability, the teacher in a looping classroom has the opportunity to participate in intervention decisions that can be incorporated into the second year of instruction, keeping the child with his or her peers while providing the special help he or she needs.

---

* From *Our Best Advice: The Multiage Problem Solving Handbook*, by Jim Grant, Bob Johnson, and Irv Richardson. Peterborough, NH: Crystal Springs Books, 1996.

Q. Are there conflicting education concepts that cancel the benefits of looping?

A. Yes. Schools often find themselves in the position of having to implement several educational concepts at once. Some of these can really get in the way of implementing looping as an effective strategy. They include:

- departmentalization. This creates a situation where students are faced with dealing with several teachers over a two- or three-year period, as opposed to one teacher. This cancels the benefit of having one adult on a consistent basis for multiple years.

  Some middle schools* have created two- and three-person teaching teams which deal with a relatively small group of students over a period of two or more years. This combines the benefits of students having long-term relationships with caring adults with much of the expertise in terms of subject matter that would otherwise be provided by the departmentalized structure.

- rigid grade-level promotion standards. Some districts have very strict guidelines for who should and should not be retained; teachers may find that some children who are lagging behind and who could benefit from the extra time provided by looping don't meet the requirements for promotion, and thus are frozen out of the looping program.

- rigid grade-specific content standards. If a district's curriculum requirements are rigid and grade-specific, it won't necessarily get in the way of looping, but it will certainly hamper flexibility and enrichment possibilities in terms of making curriculum adaptations for a two-year classroom.

---

* See *The Looping Handbook,* pp. 95-100; see also George, Paul S.; Spruel, Melody; and Moorefield, Jane. *Lincoln Middle School: A Case Study in Long-term Relationships.* Columbus, OH: The National Middle School Association, 1987.

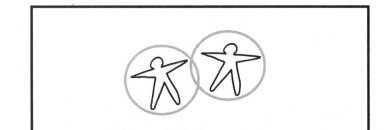

I Need Details — How Do I Implement Looping?

Q.

What are the first steps to creating a looping classroom?

A. Looping is a fairly simple practice that doesn't require the planning that other, more complex concepts require. There are a few things you should do before you begin looping.

Read all you can about looping. There are a number of magazine articles, as well as a few books, that address looping. (See the resources section, page 109.)

Arrange to visit a school and observe a looping class in action. Make sure you find an opportunity to speak to teachers who have looped, as well as administration and support staff, such as principals, superintendents, guidance counselors, special education people, etc. These people can give you a realistic view of what to expect from looping, as well as the insights they've gained from resolving difficulties in implementing looping. Good questions to ask teachers are:

- Did you enjoy having the same students for two years?
- How have the students benefited from the multiyear relationship?
- What has the parent response been?
- Has your relationship with the parents changed?
- Did you like working with the same group of parents over two years?
- How much work was involved in shifting to the multiyear configuration? Was it a positive experience? Why?
- Did you enjoy working with children at a different developmental stage than you're used to?
- What problems came up in shifting to looping? How did you solve them?
- What would you do differently another time?
- Do you plan to loop again?

Work out an agreement with your looping partner that covers all bases. When you decide to loop, you must realize that in a very real sense you become partners with the individual alternating the classes with you. You need to work out an agreement that considers all eventualities:

- What happens if, at the end of the first year, one of you decides not to loop?
- What happens in the second year if the teacher who has looped to the higher grade decides she or he wants to remain at that grade?

Develop guidelines for discipline, "opt out" possibilities (see pages 24 and 25), teacher-student conflict resolution, special education referral, assessment, and other issues that may conceivably pop up during your two-year classroom.

Talk to the parents of your students. Inform the parents of your decision, and give them the opportunity to ask questions and provide input. Also inform them of the guidelines you've created ahead of time, and assure them of the options they have in case they feel the looping structure is not working for their child.

Make sure you plan the staff development opportunities that you need. You probably already have a lot of the knowledge you need to optimize looping. As a multiyear teacher, it would be valuable to be familiar with the following practices and strategies:

- the change process
- cooperative learning
- conflict resolution
- literature-based reading
- the writing process
- thematic teaching
- learning centers
- different learning and reading styles
- multiple intelligences
- authentic assessment
- manipulative math
- hands-on science/social studies

Familiarize yourself with the curriculum requirements of both grades you plan to teach. This may include grade-specific requirements, such as health, sex education, drug awareness, and other mandated instruction. (See page 52 for ways to blend your curriculum over two years.)

Balance your classroom population as you draw up class rosters for the upcoming year. You will raise your chances of success tremendously if you start out your first year with a balanced, diverse class of students. (See pages 87-88 for criteria.)

Q.

How much lead time is needed before implementing looping?

A. It will depend on your own unique situation. It can take anywhere from a few months to a school year to fully plan your looping program. A decision to loop can be made during the spring prior to beginning the first year of the looping class, as long as you have time to implement the planning discussed on pages 74-75. This procedure can also be addressed in the fall of the first year, allowing a full year to do planning and provide parent education on looping.

This is markedly different from multiage, which takes at least a full year before beginning, and can take as much as five years to fully implement. This is largely due to the need for comprehensive training, and the complexity of blending curriculum for a group of kids of mixed ages, abilities, and grade levels.

A. Absolutely not. Looping is a very cost-effective reform which doesn't require money for expensive alterations to the physical plant, or for complex research and planning. A few expenses should be planned for, such as:

- paid leave time to allow teachers to visit looping classrooms and to visit the next grade level.

- paid staff development time to allow teachers to receive appropriate training in curriculum and instruction, as well as learning about the stages of child development.

- paid planning time.

- some additional money for research, instructional materials, professional books, and videos.

- money for hotel accommodations, travel expenses, and workshop fees.

Q.

Is looping an expensive education concept to implement?

Q.

Will looping save money?

 A. Possibly some in the long run, but this is not a valid reason to promote looping. Some money might be saved if:

- looping results in fewer special education referrals and fewer retentions.
- teacher attendance improves (see pages 31 and 48) — the district will save money on substitutes.
- student attendance improves, which is often the case. In this instance, the school's funding may improve, since funding is often based on average daily attendance.

We cannot say this strongly enough, however — looping is an educational reform, not an economic one. It should be promoted because of its benefits to students, not because of its effect on the school budget. To do otherwise will set up unrealistic expectations and possible loss of the practice if the expected financial benefits don't materialize.

A. They do surprisingly well, in most cases. Teachers have found that new students coming into the second year of a two-year class are very quickly brought up to speed by the veterans of the class, and are made to feel at home. The level of acceptance engendered by students toward each other in this atmosphere seems to easily extend itself to newcomers.

Of course, the dynamics are affected by the number of new students that enter a particular class; the more new students, the more adjustments that will have to be made. Some teachers have found that, when faced with a large group of new students coming into a class which has already been together for a year, it has taken a lot of effort and creativity to blend what is essentially two separate groups of students into one cohesive group.

High transciency rates for students are a major factor in many school districts in this country. While a large turnover in the student population is a problem for any classroom (and may in some instances lessen the effectiveness of the looping configuration), it does seem that, given the welcoming nature of the looping classroom, and with the addition of acceptance activities and opportunities for cooperative learning, looping goes a long way toward dealing with the problems in learning created by a highly mobile population.

Q.

Do transient students do well in looping classrooms?

Q.

Has looping been questioned by any special interest groups?

A. Not to the authors' knowledge, although many education reforms *have* been attacked by special interest groups. These include: critical thinking, multicultural education, cooperative learning, whole language, tolerance education, year-round schools, and multiage education.

Words are open to interpretation, and can be a source of great misunderstanding. One phrase used a lot in looping that could possibly be open to criticism is "family grouping," since classrooms who stay together with the same teacher over two years do become like a family. This phrase might evoke an emotional response from those who do not understand its meaning.

We feel that one way to avoid this criticism is to bring parents in as welcome and powerful participants in the looping classroom. This tends to happen very naturally with looping.

The Association for School Curriculum and Development (ASCD) has an easy-to-read 37-page booklet, *How to Deal With Community Criticism of School Change,* * which helps deal with these issues. It discusses how to develop a communications strategy, build support, talk about restructuring, communicate effectively, work with the media, and deal with intense criticism.

---

* Ledell, Marjorie, and Arnsparger, Arleen. *How to Deal with Community Criticism of School Change.* Alexandria, VA: Association for Supervision and Curriculum Development, 1993.

A. No. Mandating looping (or any education reform) creates problems on several levels:

- Mandates can turn resistant teachers into potential enemies of your reform.
- Not all teachers or students will benefit from any one reform.
- Mandating looping for everyone eliminates the option of choice, which is an important benefit to offer to parents.
- Mandating reforms can be a red flag for special interest groups, who may end up targeting you for criticism.

Q.

If looping is so effective, should we mandate it for every child in every school?

In Bruce Miller's book, *Children at the Center*, the author states that "there is no single right model or recipe for becoming a multiage classroom or school." (p. 103) This is true for any reform. Schools must decide what is appropriate for their own unique settings. When planning a looping program, schools should consider their own staff, student population, parents, culture, and community. Decisions about looping configurations and timelines for implementation will vary from school to school.

Change should be viewed as a process, and a transition period should be part of any effective action plan being developed by school staff. A number of schools are incorporating choices into their classroom configurations. Student populations are diverse in nature, representing different cultural and economic backgrounds, differing levels of educational experience, and a wide range of strengths and abilities. It would be naive to assume that a single classroom configuration is best for every child.

We also need to offer parents a say in their child's education, and a choice of classroom configurations is one way to empower parents and respect their views. This in turn will engender support among parents for decisions made by school administrations.

Having said that, mandates happen. One highly successful school system loops throughout the district, from grades one through eight. Looping has been mandated since the beginning of the third looping cycle. Here, looping was (and should be) an evolution, not a revolution. A few teachers ultimately left the district rather than loop, but most stayed; and with a lot of administrative support for training in instructional strategies, plus creative teaming efforts, the vast majority of teachers in the district now enthusiastically support looping.

Q.

Can looping occur at any grade level?

 A. Yes; looping has been implemented successfully from kindergarten through eighth grade. One school system has two-year teaching assignments in grades one through eight, and is looking into the possibility of applying the concept to high school in some way.

The Waldorf schools, private schools based on the anthroposophic teachings of philosopher Rudolf Steiner, have successfully educated children who stay with the same teacher from grades one through eight.

Other countries, including Japan, Germany, Israel, and Denmark practice student-teacher progression to different degrees.

A. This practice is called interbuilding looping. A good example of this is when a fourth-grade teacher in a K-4 elementary school moves to the fifth grade in a middle school. This provides the stability of the long-term teacher-student relationship and keeps the class together as a unit of close-knit friends.

This eases what can be a very stressful, difficult transition for many kids. Students moving into middle school are often moving to a larger school, probably joining students from other parts of the district, and in all likelihood are going from hands-on, manipulative, experiential learning to a concept-driven, paper and pencil curriculum — a lot of changes for ten- and eleven-year-olds to handle.

Q. I've heard of teachers looping between buildings; how does that work?

There are some problems with interbuilding looping that need to be considered:

- Many teachers don't want to change buildings, which would mean losing contact with colleagues and friends.
- Looping between buildings means dealing with two different administrative styles and philosophies that may not be compatible with each other or with the teacher's approach.
- The elementary school may be child-centered, while the middle school may be teacher-centered. The teacher may not feel comfortable with that shift in perspective.
- Class size may increase when moving from elementary school to middle school. This will affect the class in a couple ways; the most obvious is that the teacher will simply have more students to teach. The less obvious effect is that the increase in class size will necessitate adding students to the classroom who were not involved in the fourth grade class. This will change the dynamics of the class as the veterans and the new students adapt to one another.

Daniel Burke, a school superintendent in Antioch, Illinois, sees this reluctance among teachers to move as a major reason that interbuilding looping doesn't happen more often. Burke's district has two teachers looping between a K-3 elementary school and a middle school which includes fourth grade. Both teachers had taught in both schools before they decided to loop, a fact that Burke credits with their comfort level with the interbuilding concept. This, combined with two school administrations working cooperatively with each other, has resulted in a very successful looping program bridging the two schools.

© Crystal Springs Books • Peterborough, NH • 1-800-321-0401

Q.

What is an ideal class size for a looping classroom?

A. The looping classroom should contain the same number of children as single-grade, single-year classrooms in the same school at the same grade level. The benefits of looping should not be used as an excuse to increase class size.

Some teachers implementing looping actually request that a few extra students be placed in their classrooms at the beginning of the cycle. They do this with the understanding that new students will be placed in other classrooms with fewer students. The purpose for this strategy is to ensure continuity while maintaining one's own fair share of students.

Of course, small class size benefits all students. According to research from Project STAR*, with small classes in grades K-2 or K-3:

- there are fewer retentions.
- there is less need for remediation and/or special education.
- behavior improves.
- achievement increases.

These benefits are the same as those attributed to looping (see pages 13-15). It stands to reason that combining the looping configuration with small class sizes could have a powerfully beneficial effect on schoolchildren.

---

* For more information on Project STAR, contact:

Project STAR
Center of Excellence for Research in Basic Skills
Tennessee State University
330 Tenth Avenue North, Suite J
Nashville, TN 37203
(615) 963-7238

Q.

What is a good
student selection
process for
a looping
classroom?

 A. First, you need to ask yourself some questions. Who is
presently involved in making
student selection decisions? Do you
have guidelines in place? Will looping
require changing those guidelines?

If you don't have guidelines, or if
they need to be revised or updated, a
team of teachers and administrators
should be formed to work on them.

Here are some considerations in
drawing up student placement
guidelines:

- Make sure you balance your classroom in terms of student population
  (see pages 87-88).
- Make sure if teachers spend time in
  the spring placing children in balanced
  classes, that those placements are not changed over the summer,
  so that teachers return to completely different groups.
- Address the placement of new and incoming students that will
  maintain balanced classrooms.
- Establish a "getting to know you" period of time, in the fall of the
  first year, and for new, incoming second-year students, to allow
  for proactive changes.
- Have an "opting-out" policy in place at the end of the first year, to
  allow parents the choice of removing their child from the looping
  classroom if they're unsatisfied with the arrangement.

Once complete, it is important that your guidelines appear in
writing, and are known and understood by teachers and parents.

A. Children learn from each other; those with lower abilities stretch to learn from the gifted and high achievers; students without disabilities learn kindness, compassion, and caring from those who do; children with behavioral problems, or who lack positive discipline training at home, learn to behave from positive peer modeling.

Balance is a good thing! When selecting children for your looping classroom, make sure you balance your student population in terms of gender, race, socioeconomic and social-emotional factors, and cognitive abilities. Children with special physical and cognitive needs should be included, but be careful not to overload your class with special-needs students. (The proportion of special-needs kids in your class should be the same as in the general population of your school.)

Q. How do I make sure I have a balanced student population for my looping classroom?

You should also consider the developmental levels of students when balancing the classroom. Make sure a range of developmental stages is represented; then be sure your curriculum plans accommodate all of these different levels. It's especially important not to have too many developmentally young children in your classroom.

In the spring, you might use the visual organizer on the following page to begin your placement process. Any process of gathering input from parents should already have taken place. The teachers from grade levels that are sending and receiving students would meet to begin the process. Suggestions for using the placement grid are:

1. Have a grid for each teacher who will be receiving students.

2. Teachers sending students should write each student's name on a Post-it™ note (yellow for boys, blue for girls) and add any additional comments that might be helpful in the placement process.

3. Teachers sending students place each student's name on the area of the grid that best reflects his or her level of social/emotional and cognitive development.

4. The grids are placed side-by-side, which allows for quick surveys for equity, balance, and potential difficulties.

After reviewing the grids and agreeing on student placement, class lists can be made.

Teacher: _____

Grade: _____

Year: _____

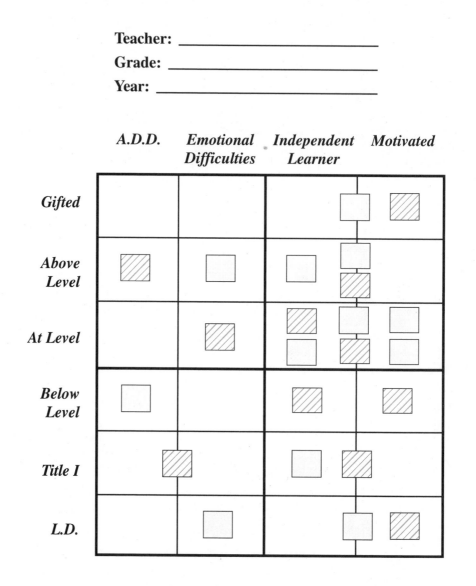

Depending on the demographics of your community, it may not be possible to balance the classroom in all respects; a community may be of predominantly one culture, or there may happen to be many children in the community with special needs. But spending time creating the best possible balance in your classroom, based on the population you have, will help you to optimize your instruction.

Q.

How do you assess your looping program?

A. To assess how you are doing, you need to reflect on the reasons you chose to implement looping, then devise the tools you will use to monitor your progress toward these goals. Identify what you will assess, your desired outcomes, how you will monitor progress, and a proposed time-line. You might follow these steps in putting together your assessment component:

First, take a sheet of paper and make four columns. Label the left-hand column "Objectives," the next column "Desired Outcomes," the third column "Assessment Tools," and the last column "Time Line."

In the "Objectives" column, list the reasons you are looping. Do you hope to strengthen student/teacher/parent relationships? to secure a more effective instructional time period? to improve attendance? to reduce special education referrals? . . . What benefits do you hope to gain by looping?

In the "Desired Outcomes" column, identify realistic benchmarks. What evidence will demonstrate that you are *progressing* toward your desired objectives? Will there be greater parental involvement, a more integrated curriculum, a higher percentage of average daily attendance?

Identify the types of tools you will use to assess your progress in the next column. Will you use anecdotal records, questionnaires, or surveys to monitor the feelings of people involved with looping? Will you use rubrics to watch your progress in your steps toward implementing the process? Will you use school records to compare daily attendance and special education referrals from year-to-year?

In the final column, set realistic dates or time periods by which you would expect to see some progress.

When developing your assessment component, build in flexibility. You might add a column for anecdotal notes, where you will write unexpected benefits or obstacles that might alter your course or time-line toward implementation. Remember — each school is unique and your assessment piece should reflect your own objectives. Revisions are a fact of life . . . expect them! Change is a process, a transition toward your destination . . . don't become overwhelmed and try to make too many changes at once! Enjoy . . . reward yourself for progress along the way, and build in fun and rest breaks to recharge your batteries along your journey!

Q.

Is chronological age at entrance a concern in a looping classroom?

A. Yes. This concern is no different for the looping classroom than for the single year, single-grade classroom. Depending on the cut-off dates for entrance in your particular school system, you could have children who are virtually a year apart in age; and chronological age is a major factor in developmental readiness.

Dr. James Uphoff, author of *Summer Children* and *Real Facts From Real Schools*, reports that children who are the youngest in a particular grade are more likely to:

- have failed a grade
- become dropouts
- be referred for testing for special services and special education
- be diagnosed as Learning Disabled
- be sent to the principal's office for discipline problems even when in high school
- be receiving various types of counseling services
- be receiving lower grades than their ability scores would indicate as reasonable
- be behind their grade peers in athletic skill level
- be chosen less frequently for leadership roles by peers or adults
- be in special service programs such as Title I
- be in speech therapy programs
- be slower in social development
- rank lower in their graduating class
- be a suicide victim
- be more of a follower than a leader
- be less attentive in class
- earn lower grades
- score lower on achievement tests.

© CRYSTAL SPRINGS BOOKS • PETERBOROUGH, NH • 1-800-321-0401

Q.

Does a looping classroom eliminate the need for a transitional kindergarten for young fives or a pre-first for young sixes?

A. No. Transitional classes are created to solve problems with developmental readiness, and looping cannot make a child grow faster, either physically or cognitively.

Many "educrats" claim that multiage education will eliminate the need for developmentally young children to take an additional year of learning time. We strongly disagree and are concerned that the same claims will be made for looping.

While looping won't eliminate the need for transitional kindergartens or pre-first grade classes, it may lower the number of children being placed in these classes. Some children, though lagging behind their classmates, need just a little extra time and attention to catch up, and the additional instructional time created in the second year through the looping structure may be just enough to let them do that.

Q.

Do you recommend looping with a pre-first grade classroom?

A. Absolutely. It could be one of the best decisions made for a group of pre-first grade children.

There is a caution, however: as high as 35 percent of children placed in a pre-first grade classroom will later be identified as having learning disabilities, attention deficit problems, or behavioral problems. Keeping a class with so many high-maintenance children together for too long could be harmful, because of the lack of modeling from more capable students.

A positive consideration about pre-first grade classes is that they are generally small. A school could decide to loop with these children, adding more children from diverse backgrounds in the second year, thereby providing the modeling opportunities these children need.

Pre-first graders tend to be needy in many ways; looping, if handled properly, would be a blessing for these children.

A. Let us give an example:
A child enters first grade, and at the end of the year is lagging behind his classmates. The teacher, recognizing that the child needs some extra help, brings him along to second grade with her, providing interventions as needed.

Toward the end of second grade, it's obvious that the interventions haven't brought the child up to speed, and he isn't ready for third grade.

Here's what happens: the teacher loops back to first grade; the second grader makes a lateral move to a new second grade situation with a new teacher, then goes on to third grade the next year. Although the child is being retained, the lateral move to a new classroom provides movement that lessens the feeling of being "kept back," and is a much kinder way of dealing with the issue than keeping the child in the same single-year classroom with the same teacher while all his friends move on without him.

Q. If a child needs to take an additional year of learning time, how would he or she do that in a looping classroom?

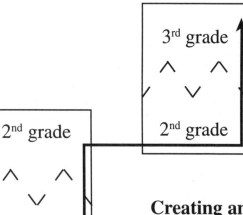

Some students may take four years to progress through three grade levels

Creating an additional year of learning time in a looping or multiage or staggered configuration

It's important to understand when grade-level retention is and isn't the proper intervention for a particular child. A child may benefit from retention when he or she is:

- chronologically too young for his or her present grade-level placement.
- developmentally too young for his or her grade or program.
- physically small for his or her age.
- immature socially and emotionally.

Children who may be harmed, rather than helped, by retention are those who are:

- slow learners.
- unmotivated students.
- emotionally disturbed.
- behavior problems.
- lagging behind because of poverty.
- linguistically different.
- lagging due to excessive absenteeism.
- children of parents opposed to grade-level retention.
- already a year older than their peers.
- too "street-wise".
- high-needs (multiple complex problems).
- suffering from low self-esteem.

Additional information on retention is included in the appendix (page 103), which contains an excerpt from *The Looping Handbook: Teachers and Students Progressing Together*. For a more comprehensive look at retention, see *Retention and Its Prevention: Making Informed Decisions About Individual Children*, by Jim Grant (Rosemont, NJ: Modern Learning Press, 1997).

A. Yes. Here's how it can be done:

A kindergarten teacher with a morning and an afternoon kindergarten chooses to loop to first grade with either the morning or afternoon group of students (or a blend of both groups). The first grade teacher moves to kindergarten to begin a new two-year cycle.

Q.

Is it possible to loop with a half-day kindergarten?

Morning Kindergarten Class — **20 Children** → 1st Grade (Loop)

Kindergarten Teacher

First grade teacher moves down

Kindergarten teacher moves up

Afternoon Kindergarten Class — **20 Children** → Conventional one year 1st grade

Here are some options:

- The morning class can loop.
- The afternoon class can loop.
- Ten students from the morning class and ten students from the afternoon class can loop.
- Twenty out of forty students from the kindergarten population can loop (chosen by random selection from the morning and afternoon classes).

Make sure if you do loop with some, but not all of your students, that the selection process is fair, and that you end up with a balanced classroom. One good way to do this is a lottery.

Q.

Can a teacher loop with a partial class?

 A. Yes, but there should be a valid reason for doing so.

The administration needs to make sure that looping with a partial class is not used as a way of avoiding high-maintenance and low-ability students.

If for some reason looping with a partial class is necessary (for instance, to deal with class size issues, high mobility rates, or demographic shifts) the teacher needs to assign a *heterogeneous* group of students, and also *keep* a heterogeneous group of students. If the student selection process somehow seems unfair, you risk alienating parents and fellow staff members.

In the event that looping with a partial class is an option, we advise that teachers and administrators discuss and agree on student selection decisions.

Q.

Is the multi-age classroom a form of looping?

A. Yes, multiage is a more complex form of the multiyear configuration; whereas looping is for the most part a single-grade, two-year teacher-student relationship, multiage adds a mixed age group of children from different grade levels.

The benefits of single-grade looping (see pages 13-15) also accrue with multiage education. The obstacles are similar, yet are frequently more complex in a multiage configuration.

Q.

Is it possible to loop with a multiage classroom?

A. Yes. Judy Boniface, an elementary school teacher in Woodinville, Washington, taught a second-third grade multiage classroom, then moved up to a third-fourth grade multiage setting with her class, and again to a fourth-fifth blended grade. She had many of her students for three years. Next year she plans to have a four/five/six multiage, with grade six being represented by one student. She is going to remain at the upper grades rather than looping back to second/third grade because of considerations involving numbers of students, rather than by choice.

"I would never want to go back to a single-age classroom," she said. "There are so many things we've accomplished that we never would have been able to do in a single-year classroom." Her students essentially run the classroom, taking attendance, assigning themselves jobs, ordering lunches, and checking in (but not correcting) their own homework.

Boniface has gone through this multiage looping structure twice. The first time, "the kids got sick of me" by the third year; for her second loop, she made sure that she made enough changes in her classroom instruction and strategies to keep things fresh.

For the upcoming school year, Boniface will be giving her fifth graders up to the teacher in the classroom next door, "because we feel they need a change," she said. However, she will be team teaching with that particular teacher, so her former students will still have plenty of contact with her.

Q.

Do you think looping is an effective steppingstone to creating a multiage classroom?

A. Absolutely. There are many similarities between multiage and looping. The teacher (or team) in both paradigms:

- works with the same group of students for a two-year period.
- can discover if he or she is comfortable working with the same parent group for two years.
- has an opportunity to work with, and possibly blend, two years of curriculums. (One of the major concerns teachers have in implementing multiage is the complexity of blending two years' worth of curriculum requirements for a mixed-age group of students. This is an excellent first step.)
- works with children at two different grade levels, who are at multiple stages of development.

A teacher who enjoys working with the looping structure may want to explore creating a truly seamless, continuous progress curriculum, and take advantage of the benefits of children of different ages and developmental stages working together — two benefits unique to multiage education.

Teachers in a looping partnership are in an ideal situation to try out multiage groupings. For example, the third and fourth grade teachers might pull their students together and team teach a few thematic units during the year. This affords the opportunity to experience the dynamics of multiage groupings while remaining in a looping configuration. Decisions about multiage can be made through hands-on, practical experience.

Q.

Does teaching a multiyear class require more than one certification?

A. That depends on the state. In some states and in some circumstances, more than one certification is required. In Florida, for instance, a teacher wanting to loop from kindergarten to first grade needs a certification in early childhood education for kindergarten and a certification in elementary education for first grade. A teacher determined to try looping may have to take extra course work to secure the second certification.

There is the possibility that a tenacious principal may be able to get the state to waive or defer multiple certification requirements; but it is wise, before deciding to loop, to check certification requirements with your state's Board of Education.

A. Yes. We feel that looping is compatible with the concept of year-round schooling. One advantage of year-round schooling is that students and teachers are never out of school for more than a few weeks, so that a momentum for learning is created. With the time-saving and relationship-building qualities of a good looping program, you can create a powerful structure that comes close to a seamless, continuous progress program.

Q.

Would looping work in a year-round school?

"Looping is a solid educational concept that would work well in a year-round school," said Bernie Hanlon, superintendent of two very successful multiage, year-round schools in California.

Hanlon's schools are single-track year-round schools; that is, all teachers and students share the same nine-weeks-in, three-weeks-out schedule. In four-track year-round schools, the student population is divided into four groups; three groups are in school, and one is out of school, at any particular time. Hanlon doesn't have personal experience with four-track schools, but "foresees no problems" with looping in either a single-track or four-track school.

For more information on year-round education, contact:

> National Association for Year-Round Education (NAYRE)
> P.O. Box 711386
> San Diego, CA 92171-1386
> (619) 276-5296

Q.

Is it difficult for a principal to run a school with both looping and single-year classrooms?

A. Yes, it can be. Providing a choice of programs can be a great way of garnering parent support, but it's a lot more complex at an administrative level. The principal has to be the guiding spirit behind any changes in the school, and juggling a number of different programs can be difficult at an organizational level, as well as at an interpersonal level with the staff.

An increasing number of schools that practice looping also do multiage and single-year, single-grade classes. Making sure all programs receive the proper support and encouragement, and avoiding staff dissension among the teachers of various programs, can be an exercise in diplomacy.

To see more about avoiding staff dissension, see pages 59-60.

Appendix

Retention —
A High-Stakes Decision

O ne of the most critical decisions a teacher has to make is whether to promote or retain a child who is not succeeding in school. While looping certainly reduces the need for grade-level retention, it does not entirely eliminate it.

The issue of whether to retain or socially promote a student is difficult, and is made more so because of its controversial and sometimes political nature. The National Association for the Education of Young Children (NAEYC) has taken a position against not only grade-level retention, but any form of extra time if it exceeds the traditional lock-step time frame. Many studies have been made that show negative consequences of retaining students. (On the other side, many school systems have rigid retention policies that require students to be retained based on a single factor, such as a standardized test score.)

While social promotion may be done partly to save a student the embarrassment and emotional pain of being left behind by his peers, the decision is often an economic one; that is, the school system doesn't want to pay for an extra year of schooling.

We're Retaining the Wrong Kids!

Most of the studies made on retention have two problems: they're group studies, rather than individual case studies, and they're made on a population which includes many students retained for the wrong reasons. Naturally, the results are going to be skewed.

When Retention is an Inappropriate Intervention

The children who are retained exhibit real problems that need to be addressed somehow. But many times grade-level retention is used when another intervention would be more appropriate and more effective. For the following students, retention may well be counterproductive:

• *The slower learner.* A child with a low I.Q. (a range of 70-89), who has been identified as a slower learner, usually will not benefit much from an extra year of the same curriculum with the same teacher. A more appropriate intervention may be a special-needs assessment and instructional support and adaptations as needed. Retention is not a substitute for special education!

• *An unmotivated student.* An unmotivated student will certainly not be motivated by another year of the same curriculum that bored him in the first place. Better to recognize the problem early and try to fix it; learning contracts may help, as well as thematic studies that incorporate some of the unmotivated student's interests. If the student doesn't respond to coaching or encouragement whatsoever, it might be wise to look at underlying causes for the lack of motivation.

• *An emotionally disturbed child.* Counseling, and in some severe cases, special placement, would be more appropriate than grade-level retention. Retention in this case may only add more pressure and stress to the child's life.

Be aware that some children show signs of emotional distress when they are in over their heads academically or socially in school. This is a readiness issue, which *can* usually be addressed by more learning time in a grade.

• *A child with a behavior disorder.* Again, counseling, and possibly a different approach to in-class rules of behavior would be appropriate.

• *A child raised in poverty.* Enrichment activities, acceleration, and tutoring may be more appropriate to make up for a lack of resources at home. (Be aware that a background of poverty often creates readiness issues.)

• *A linguistically different child.* A child who cannot understand what's going on in class because of a language barrier is not going to understand it the second time around, without help. A better intervention would be a good ESL (English as a Second Language) program which supports the child's studies while teaching the child English.

• *A child who has a history of excessive absenteeism.* This is a usually a parental issue, not the child's issue, and needs to be worked out with the parents or guardian.

Sometimes excessive absenteeism may be because the child's family moves frequently. Grade-level retention won't help here; possibly assessment of academic needs and individualized instruction and tutoring might. This is a tough issue. Teachers have to reconcile themselves to doing the best they can with transient students while they have them and, unfortunately, let go when the students are gone. (An aside — if outgoing students can be packed off with lots of authentic assessment of their capabilities for their next teacher, they will have a head start on their next school assignment.)

A long period of absence caused by a student's illness, or injury in an accident, is different. Grade-level retention may be appropriate under these circumstances depending on the length of the student's absence from school.

• *A child whose parents are opposed to extra time through grade-level retention.* Parents have very strong feelings about retention, on both sides of the issue. Some parents will be very adamant about their child's not staying back. Forced retention against parents' wishes never works.

• *A child who is already a year older than his peers.* Placing a child in a single-grade classroom with children two years younger than he will isolate him from children his own age and create a peer group for him that is very much younger than him developmentally. The child's self-esteem will suffer.

Students who are much older than their classmates are at high risk for dropping out of school.

• *A child who is too "street wise" for her age.* This is for the benefit of the children coming into the class — they don't need to learn what this student can teach them; and retention will not bring this student back to an age of innocence.

• *A child who has a multitude of complex problems (high-impact child).* When a child is exposed to many risk factors — for instance, coming from poverty, from a single-parent family, with health problems — each problem interacts with every other problem, making each one impact more strongly on the child. A grade-level retention for such a highly-impacted child will probably add more stress to an already burdensome situation. This child and his or her family need to be connected with as many support services as necessary.

• *A child with very low self-esteem.* This child could be devastated by grade-level retention. Often it is better to socially promote, while supporting the child's academics and social/emotional needs.

Be aware of the fact that children placed in the wrong grade exhibit signs of low self-esteem. Assess the child's developmental readiness and current grade placement; if it is determined that a lack of readiness is the issue here, moving the child back to a lower grade, or retaining the child, may solve the problem.

Retention and Readiness

Grade-level retention is most often the appropriate intervention to correct wrong grade placement. A good candidate for retention may be:

• chronologically too young for his/her present grade-level placement.
• developmentally too young for his/her grade or program.
• physically small for his or her age.

The child should be of average or above-average intelligence, without apparent learning disabilities, and be in the same age range as his or her current peer group (within a year of being the same age.)

The parents must strongly support grade-level retention for their child, and the child must be able to accept it as well. (In some instances, children have asked to be allowed to stay in the same grade for a second year; this request should be honored if possible.)

Do It Early

If a child needs more time in a grade, do it in the early childhood years — and don't hesitate to change a child's placement midyear if necessary. When a child is in the wrong grade, it's evident from the outset. Making a child struggle through three years of schooling and delaying a decision to retain until third grade will cause the child years of unnecessary frustration, and will batter his or her self-esteem. Retention on top of all this will be a hard blow.

If you do have to retain an older student, do it only with his or her unconditional support.

Making the Decision

Don't ever make a decision to retain a student unilaterally. This decision should involve the classroom teacher, the principal, any support staff and specialists involved, and the parents.

The decision to retain should be made based on many factors, not on a single test score or some other isolated event. Where another, less drastic intervention may resolve a student's school problems, that strategy should be used.

Retention Plus

Keeping a student in the same grade for two years will not magically solve the student's academic problems. A teacher needs to explore instructional strategies that will work better with this student than the ones that failed the student the previous year. (If a particular approach didn't work the first time, it probably won't work the second.)

Make sure that remedial and support services are provided as needed. Be aware that, even if a child is retained because of a readiness issue, he or she may have other difficulties, like learning problems, that need to be addressed.

Looping and Retention

As we said at the beginning of the chapter, looping can reduce, but not eliminate grade-level retention. The advantage of looping is that the teacher has two years to observe and get to know each student, two years to identify and assess potential problems, and two years to implement instructional strategies and apply interventions to resolve any problems that may exist.

With borderline students — those students who may not need a full year, but just a little extra time and attention — that may be enough. When developmentally young students have serious difficulty after two years in a multiyear classroom, grade-level retention should be considered when, and only when, all other options have been tried. Retention is a necessary tool, but it should be the intervention of last resort.

---

* From *The Looping Handbook: Students and Teachers Progressing Together.* by Jim Grant, Bob Johnson, and Irv Richardson. Peterborough, NH: Crystal Springs Books, 1996.

Resources

Looping and Related Topics

Burke, Daniel L. "Multi-Year Teacher/Student Relationships Are a Long-Overdue Arrangement," *Phi Delta Kappan*, January 1996.

ERS Info-File #285.0. "Persistence Teams/Looping." This is a collection of articles about multiyear assignments and related topics; many of the articles are about Waldorf schools. Contact: Educational Research Service, 2000 Clarendon Blvd., Arlington, VA 22201 Phone: 703-243-2100; FAX 703-243-8316; e-mail: ers@access.digex.net

Forsten, Char. *The Multiyear Lesson Plan Book.* Peterborough, NH: Crystal Springs Books, 1996.

George, Paul S.; Spruel, Melody; and Moorefield, Jane. *Lincoln Middle School; A Case Study in Long-term Relationships.* Columbus, OH: National Middle School Association, 1987.

Glover, Mary Kenner. *Two Years: A Teacher's Memoir.* Portsmouth, NH: Heinemann, 1993.

Grant, Jim. *The Looping Classroom.* (Video) Peterborough, NH: Crystal Springs Books, 1996.

Grant, Jim; Johnson, Bob; and Richardson, Irv. *The Looping Handbook: Teachers and Students Progressing Together.* Peterborough, NH: Crystal Springs Books, 1996.

Hanson, Barbara. "Getting to Know You: Multiyear Teaching," *Educational Leadership,* November, 1995.

Jacoby, Deborah. "Twice the Learning and Twice the Love." *Teaching K-8,* March 1994.

Jankowsky, Elizabeth, Ed.D. "The Perception of the Effects of Looping on Classroom Relationships and Community in Learning." Doctoral dissertation for University of Sarasota, 1996.

Mazzuchi, Diana, and Brooks, Nancy. "The Gift of Time." *Teaching K-8,* February, 1992.

Million, June. "To Loop or Not to Loop? This is a Question for Many Schools." *NAESP Communicator,* Vol. 18, Number 6, February 1996.

Rappa, Joseph B. "Presentation to the National Education Commission on Time and Learning," Cambridge, MA, September 24, 1993.

Other Topics of Interest to Multiyear Teachers

Assessment

Batzle, Janine. *Portfolio Assessment and Evaluation: Developing and Using Portfolios in the K-6 Classroom.* Cypress, CA: Creative Teaching Press, 1992.

Belanoff, Pat, and Dickson, Marcia, eds. *Portfolios: Process and Product.* Portsmouth, NH: Heinemann, 1991.

Clay, Marie. *An Observation Survey of Early Literacy Achievement.* Portsmouth, NH: Heinemann, 1993.

―――. *Sand* and *Stones: "Concepts about Print" Tests.* Portsmouth, NH: Heinemann, 1980.

Clemmons, J., Laase, L., Cooper, D., Areglado, N., and Dill, M. *Portfolios in the Classroom: A Teacher's Sourcebook.* New York: Scholastic, Inc., 1993.

Daly, Elizabeth, ed. *Monitoring Children's Language Development.* Portsmouth, NH: Heinemann, 1992.

Graves, Donald, and Sustein, Bonnie, eds. *Portfolio Portraits.* Portsmouth, NH: Heinemann, 1992.

Harp, Bill, ed. *Assessment and Evaluation in Whole Language Programs.* Norwood, MA: Christopher Gordon Publishers, 1993.

Lazear, David. *Multiple Intelligence Approaches to Assessment: Solving the Assessment Conundrum.* Palatine, IL: IRI/Skylight Publishing, Inc., 1994.

Parsons, Les. *Response Journals.* Portsmouth, NH: Heinemann, 1989.

Picciotto, Linda. *Evaluation: A Team Effort.* Ont.: Scholastic, 1992.

Behavior/Discipline

Albert, Linda. *An Administrator's Guide to Cooperative Discipline.* Circle Pines, MN: American Guidance Service, 1989.

―――. *Cooperative Discipline: How to Manage Your Classroom and Promote Self-Esteem.* Circle Pines, MN: American Guidance Service, 1996.

―――. *Cooperative Discipline Elementary Kit.* (Three-video series, Implementation Guide, ten color posters, *Cooperative Discipline* book). Circle Pines, MN: American Guidance Service, 1996.

―――. *Linda Albert's Advice for Coping With Kids.* Tampa, FL: Alkorn House, 1992.

―――. *Responsible Kids in School and At Home: The Cooperative Discipline Way.* (Six-video series). Circle Pines, MN: American Guidance Service, 1994.

Bluestein, Jane. *21st Century Discipline — Teaching Students Responsibility and Self-Control.* New York: Scholastic, 1988.

Burke, Kay. *What to Do with the Kid Who . . . Developing Cooperation, Self-Discipline and Responsibility in the Classroom.* Palatine, IL: IRI/Skylight Publishing, 1992.

Canfield, Jack, and Siccone, Frank. *101 Ways to Develop Student Self-Esteem and Responsibility.* Needham Heights, MA: Allyn & Bacon, 1993.

Charles, C.M. *Building Classroom Discipline.* New York: Longman, 1992.

Coletta, Anthony. *What's Best for Kids: A Guide to Developmentally Appropriate Practices for Teachers & Parents of Children Ages 4-8.* Rosemont, NJ: Modern Learning Press, 1991.

Curwin, Richard L., and Mendler, Allen N. *Discipline with Dignity.* Alexandria, VA: Association for Supervision and Curriculum Development, 1993.

———. *Am I in Trouble? Using Discipline to Teach Young Children Responsibility.* Santa Cruz, CA: Network Publications, 1990.

Fox, Lynn. *Let's Get Together.* Rolling Hills, CA: Jalmar Press, 1993.

Knight, Michael et al. *Teaching Children to Love Themselves.* Hillside, NJ: Vision Press, 1982.

Kohn, Alfie. *Punished by Rewards: The Trouble with Gold Stars, Incentive Plans, A's, Praise, and Other Bribes.* Boston: Houghton Mifflin, 1993.

Kreidler, William. *Creative Conflict Resolution: Strategies for Keeping Peace in the Classroom.* Glenview, IL: Scott, Foresman, & Co., 1984.

Mendler, Allen. *Smiling at Yourself: Educating Young Children About Stress and Self-Esteem.* Santa Cruz, CA: Network Publications, 1990.

———. *What Do I Do When? How to Achieve Discipline With Dignity in the Classroom.* Bloomington, IL: National Educational Service, 1992.

Nelson, Jane. *Positive Discipline.* New York: Ballantine Books, 1987.

Nelson, Jane; Lott, Lynn; and Glenn, Stephen. *Positive Discipline in the Classroom.* Rocklin, CA: Prima Publishing, 1993.

Redenbach, Sandi. *Self-Esteem: The Necessary Ingredient for Success.* Esteem Seminar Publications, 1991.

Reider, Barbara. *A Hooray Kind of Kid.* Folsom, CA: Sierra House Publishing, 1988.

Vail, Priscilla. *Emotion: The On-Off Switch for Learning.* Rosemont, NJ: Modern Learning Press, 1994.

Wright, Esther. *Good Morning, Class — I Love You!* Rolling Hills, CA: Jalmar Press, 1988.

———. *Loving Discipline A to Z.* San Francisco: Teaching From the Heart, 1994.

Cooperative Learning

Cohen, Dorothy. *Designing Groupwork: Strategies for the Heterogeneous Classroom.* New York: Teachers College Press, 1994.

Curran, Lorna. *Cooperative Learning Lessons for Little Ones: Literature-Based Language Arts & Social Skills.* San Juan Capistrano, CA: Resources for Teachers, Inc., 1992.

DeBolt, Virginia, with Dr. Spencer Kagan. *Write! Cooperative Learning and The Writing Process.* San Juan Capistrano, CA: Kagan Cooperative Learning, 1994.

Ellis, Susan S., and Whalen, Susan F. *Cooperative Learning: Getting Started.* New York: Scholastic, 1990.

Fisher, Bobbi. *Thinking and Learning Together: Curriculum and Community in a Primary Classroom.* Portsmouth, NH: Heinemann, 1995.

Forte, Imogene, and MacKenzie, Joy. *The Cooperative Learning Guide and Planning Pak for Primary Grades: Thematic Projects and Activities.* Nashville, TN: Incentive Publications, 1992.

Glover, Mary, and Sheppard, Linda. *Not on Your Own: The Power of Learning Together.* New York: Scholastic, 1990.

Johnson, David, and Johnson, Roger. *Cooperation and Competition: Theory and Research.* Edina, MN: Interaction Book Company, 1989.

———. *Learning Together and Alone.* Englewood Cliffs, NJ: Prentice Hall, Inc., 1991.

Kagan, Spencer. *Cooperative Learning.* San Juan Capistrano, CA: Resources for Teachers, Inc., 1994.

Reid, Jo Anne; Forrestal, P.; and Cook, J. *Small Group Learning in the Classroom.* Portsmouth, NH: Heinemann, 1989.

Shaw, Vanston, with Spencer Kagan, Ph.D. *Communitybuilding In the Classroom.* San Juan Capistrano, CA: Kagan Cooperative Learning, 1992.

Slavin, Robert. *Cooperative Learning.* Englewood Cliffs, NJ: Prentice Hall, 1989.

———. *Cooperative Learning.* Boston: Allyn and Bacon, 1995.

Curriculum — Overview

Bredekamp, Sue, and Rosegrant, Teresa, eds. *Reaching Potentials: Appropriate Curriculum and Assessment for Young Children, Vol. 1.* Washington, DC: NAEYC, 1992.

Cummings, Carol, Ph.D. *Managing to Teach: A Guide to Classroom Management.* (2nd edition) Edmonds, WA: Teaching, Inc., 1996.

Dodge, Diane Trister; Jablon, Judy R.; and Bickart, Toni S. *Constructing Curriculum for the Primary Grades.* Washington, DC: Teaching Strategies, Inc., 1994.

Fogarty, Robin. *The Mindful School: How to Integrate the Curricula.* Palatine, IL: Skylight Publishing, 1991.

Hall, G.E., and Loucks, S.F. "Program Definition and Adaptation: Implications for Inservice." *Journal of Research and Development in Education* (1981) 14, 2:46-58.

Hohmann, C. *Mathematics: High Scope K-3 Curriculum Guide.* (Illustrated field test edition.) Ypsilanti, MI: High Scope Press, 1991.

Maehr, J. *Language and Literacy: High Scope K-3 Curriculum Guide.* (Illustrated field test edition.) Ypsilanti, MI: High Scope Press, 1991.

National Association of Elementary School Principals. *Standards for Quality Elementary and Middle Schools: Kindergarten through Eighth Grade.* Alexandria, VA, 1990.

Short, Kathy, and Burke, Carolyn. *Creating Curriculum.* Portsmouth, NH: Heinemann, 1981.

Rowan, Thomas E., and Morrow, Lorna J. *Implementing the K-8 Curriculum and Evaluation Standards: Readings from the "Arithmetic Teacher."* Reston, VA: National Council of Teachers of Mathematics, 1993.

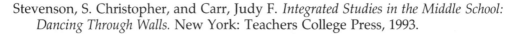
Stevenson, S. Christopher, and Carr, Judy F. *Integrated Studies in the Middle School: Dancing Through Walls.* New York: Teachers College Press, 1993.

Whitin, D.; Mills, H.; and O'Keefe, T. *Living and Learning Mathematics: Stories and Strategies for Supporting Mathematical Literacy.* Portsmouth, NH: Heinemann, 1990.

Curriculum — Integrated Activities

Bauer, Karen, and Drew, Rosa. *Alternatives to Worksheets.* Cypress, CA: Creative Teaching Press, 1992.

Beierle, Marlene, and Lynes, Teri. *Book Cooks: Literature-Based Classroom Cooking (4-6).* Cypress, CA: Creative Teaching Press, 1992.

Brainard, Audrey, and Wrubel, Denise H. *Literature-Based Science Activities: An Integrated Approach.* New York: Scholastic, 1993.

Bruno, Janet. *Book Cooks: Literature-Based Classroom Cooking. (K-3).* Cypress, CA: Creative Teaching Press, 1991.

Burns, Marilyn. *About Teaching Mathematics.* Sausalito, CA: Math Solutions Publications, 1992.

————. *A Collection of Math Lessons: From Grades 3 Through 6.* White Plains: Cuisinaire Company of America, 1987.

Burns, Marilyn, and Tank, B. *A Collection of Math Lessons: From Grades 1 Through 3.* White Plains: Cuisinaire Company of America, 1987.

Cherkerzian, Diane. *The Complete Lesson Plan Book.* Peterborough, NH: Crystal Springs Books, 1993.

Forsten, Char. *Teaching Thinking and Problem Solving in Math.* New York: Scholastic Professional Books, 1992.

————. *Using Calculators is Easy!* New York: Scholastic Professional Books, 1992.

Goin, Kenn; Ripp, Eleanor; and Solomon, Kathleen Nastasi. *Bugs to Bunnies: Hands-on Animal Science Activities for Young Children.* New York: Chatterbox Press, 1989.

Hiatt, Catherine; Wolven, Doug; Botka, Gwen; and Richmond, Jennifer. *More Alternatives to Worksheets.* Cypress, CA: Creative Teaching Press, 1994.

Huck, Charlotte, and Hickman, Janet, eds. *The Best of the Web.* Columbus, OH: Ohio State University, 1982.

Irvine, Joan. *How to Make Pop-ups.* New York: Beech Tree Books, 1987.

————. *How to Make Super Pop-ups.* New York: Beech Tree Books, 1992.

Johnson, Virginia. *Hands-On Math: Manipulative Activities for the Classroom.* Cypress, CA: Creative Teaching Press, 1994.

Jorgensen, Karen. *History Workshop.* Portsmouth, NH: Heinemann, 1993.

Kohl, MaryAnn, and Potter, Jean. *ScienceArts: Discovering Science Through Art Experiences.* Bellingham, WA: Bright Ring Publishing, 1993.

McCarthy, Tara. *Literature-Based Geography Activities: An Integrated Approach.* New York: Scholastic, 1992.

Ritter, Darlene. *Literature-Based Art Activities (K-3).* Cypress, CA: Creative Teaching Press, 1992.

———. *Literature-Based Art Activities (4-6).* Cypress, CA: Creative Teaching Press, 1992.

Rothstein, Gloria Lesser. *From Soup to Nuts: Multicultural Cooking Activities and Recipes.* New York: Scholastic, 1994.

Ruef, Kerry. *The Private Eye. Looking/Thinking by Analogy: A Guide to Developing the Interdisciplinary Mind.* Seattle: The Private Eye Project, 1992.

Spann, Mary Beth. *Literature-Based Multicultural Activities.* New York: Scholastic, 1992.

———. *Literature-Based Seasonal and Holiday Activities.* New York: Scholastic, 1991.

Developmental Education / Readiness

Boyer, Ernest. *The Basic School: A Community for Learning.* Ewing, NJ: Carnegie Foundation for the Advancement of Learning, 1995.

———. *Ready to Learn: A Mandate for the Nation.* Princeton, NJ: The Foundation for the Advancement of Teaching, 1991.

Brazelton, T. Berry. *To Listen to a Child: Understanding the Normal Problems of Growing Up.* Reading, MA: Addison-Wesley, 1986.

———. *Touchpoints: The Essential Reference. Your Child's Emotional and Behavioral Development.* Reading, MA: Addison-Wesley, 1994.

———. *Working and Caring.* Reading, MA: Addison-Wesley, 1985.

Bredekamp, Sue, ed. *Developmentally Appropriate Practice in Early Childhood Programs,* revised edition. Washington, DC: National Association for the Education of Young Children, 1997.

Charney, Ruth Sidney. *Teaching Children to Care: Management in the Responsive Classroom.* Greenfield, MA: Northeast Foundation for Children, 1991.

Coletta, Anthony. *Kindergarten Readiness Checklist for Parents.* Rosemont, NJ: Modern Learning Press, 1991.

Elovson, Allanna. *The Kindergarten Survival Book.* Santa Monica, CA: Parent Ed Resources, 1991.

Grant, Jim. *Developmental Education in the 1990's.* Rosemont, NJ: Modern Learning Press, 1991.

———. *"I Hate School!" Some Common Sense Answers for Educators and Parents Who Want to Know Why & What To Do About It.* Rosemont, NJ: Programs for Education, 1994.

———. *Jim Grant's Book of Parent Pages.* Rosemont, NJ: Programs for Education, 1988.

———. *Retention and Its Prevention: Making Informed Decisions About Individual Children.* Rosemont, NJ: Modern Learning Press, 1997.

Grant, Jim, and Azen, Margot. *Every Parent's Owner's Manuals. (Three-, Four-, Five-, Six-, Seven-Year- Old).* Rosemont, NJ: Programs for Education.

Hayes, Martha, and Faggella, Kathy. *Think It Through.* Bridgeport CT: First Teacher Press, 1986.

Healy, Jane M. *Endangered Minds: Why Children Don't Think and What We Can Do About It.* New York: Simon and Schuster, 1990.

———. *Your Child's Growing Mind: A Guide to Learning and Brain Development From Birth to Adolescence.* New York: Doubleday, 1987.

Holt, John. *How Children Fail.* New York: Dell Publishing, 1964, 1982.

Horowitz, Janet, and Faggella, Kathy. *Partners for Learning.* Bridgeport, CT: First Teacher Press, 1986.

Karnofsky, Florence, and Weiss, Trudy. *How To Prepare Your Child for Kindergarten.* Carthage, IL: Fearon Teacher Aids, 1993.

Lamb, Beth, and Logsdon, Phyllis. *Positively Kindergarten: A Classroom-Proven, Theme-based Developmental Guide for the Kindergarten Teacher.* Rosemont, NJ: Modern Learning Press, 1991.

Mallory, Bruce, and New, Rebecca, eds. *Diversity and Developmentally Appropriate Practices: Challenges for Early Childhood Education.* New York: Teachers College Press, 1994.

Miller, Karen. *Ages and Stages: Developmental Descriptions and Activities Birth Through Eight Years.* Chelsea, MA: Telshare Publishing Co., 1985.

National Association of Elementary School Principals. *Early Childhood Education and the Elementary School Principal.* Alexandria, VA: NAESP, 1990.

National Association of State Boards of Education. *Right From the Start: The Report of the NASBE Task Force on Early Childhood Education.* Alexandria, VA: NASBE, 1988.

Northeast Foundation for Children. *A Notebook for Teachers: Making Changes in the Elementary Curriculum.* Greenfield, MA, 1993.

Reavis, George H. *The Animal School.* Rosemont, NJ: Modern Learning Press, 1988.

Singer, Dorothy, and Revenson, Tracy. *How a Child Thinks: A Piaget Primer.* Independence, MO: International University Press, 1978.

Uphoff, James K. *Real Facts From Real Schools: What You're Not Supposed To Know About School Readiness and Transition Programs.* Rosemont, NJ: Modern Learning Press, 1995.

Uphoff, James, K.; Gilmore, June; and Huber, Rosemarie. *Summer Children: Ready (or Not) for School.* Middletown, OH: The Oxford Press, 1986.

Wood, Chip. *Yardsticks: Children in the Classroom Ages 4-14.* Greenfield, MA: Northeast Foundation for Children, 1996.

Inclusion / Differently-Abled / Learning Disabilities

Dudley-Marling, Curtis. *When School is a Struggle.* New York: Scholastic, 1990.

Bailey, D.B, and Wolery, M. *Teaching Infants and Preschoolers with Handicaps.* Columbus, OH: Merrill, 1984.

Dunn, Kathryn B., and Dunn, Allison B. *Trouble with School: A Family Story about Learning Disabilities.* Rockville, MD: Woodbine House, 1993.

Fagan, S.A.; Graves, D.L.; and Tressier-Switlick, D. *Promoting Successful Mainstreaming: Reasonable Classroom Accommodations for Learning Disabled Students.* Rockville, MD: Montgomery County Public Schools, 1984.

Friend, Marilyn, and Cook, Lynne. "The New Mainstreaming." *Instructor Magazine,* (March 1992): 30-35.

Goodman, Gretchen. *I Can Learn! Strategies and Activities for Gray-Area Children.* Peterborough, NH: Crystal Springs Books, 1995.

———. *Inclusive Classrooms from A to Z: A Handbook for Educators.* Columbus, OH: Teachers' Publishing Group, 1994.

Harwell, Joan. *Complete Learning Disabilities Handbook.* New York: Simon & Schuster, 1989.

Jenkins, J., and Jenkins, L. "Peer Tutoring in Elementary and Secondary Programs." In *Effective Strategies for Exceptional Children,* edited by Meyer, E.L.; Vergason, G.A.; and Whelan, R.J., 335-354, Denver, CO: Love Publishing Co., 1988.

Lang, Greg and Berberich, Chris. *All Children are Special: Creating an Inclusive Classroom.* York, ME: Stenhouse Publishers, 1995.

McGregor, G., and Vogelsberg, R.T. *Transition Needs Assessment for Parents.* Philadelphia, PA: Temple University, 1989.

Perske, R. and Perske, M. *Circle of Friends.* Nashville, TN: Abingdon Press, 1988.

Phinney, Margaret. *Reading with the Troubled Reader.* Portsmouth, NH: Heinemann, 1989.

Rainforth, Beverly; York, Jennifer; and McDonald, Cathy. *Collaborative Teams for Students with Severe Disabilities.* Baltimore: Paul H. Brookes, 1992.

Rhodes, Lynn, and Dudley-Marling, Curtis. *Readers and Writers with a Difference: A Holistic Approach to Teaching Learning Disabled and Remedial Students.* Portsmouth: Heinemann, 1988.

Rosner, Jerome. *Helping Children Overcome Learning Difficulties.* New York: Walker and Co., 1979.

Stainback, S., and Stainback, W. *Curriculum Considerations in Inclusive Classrooms: Facilitating Learning for All Students.* Baltimore: Paul H. Brookes, 1992.

———. *Support Networks for Inclusive Schooling.* Baltimore: Paul H. Brookes, 1990.

Stainback, S., Stainback, W., and Forest, M., eds. *Educating All Students in the Mainstream of Regular Education.* Baltimore: Paul H. Brookes, 1987.

Thousand, J., and Villa, R. "Strategies for Educating Learners with Severe Handicaps Within Their Local Home, Schools and Communities." *Focus on Exceptional Children,* 23 (3), 1-25, 1990.

Vail, Priscilla. *About Dyslexia.* Rosemont, NJ: Programs for Education, 1990.

———. *Smart Kids with School Problems.* New York: E.P. Dutton, 1987.

Vandercook, T., and York, J. "A Team Approach to Program Development and Support." In *Support Networks for Inclusive Schooling: Interdependent Integrated Education,* edited by Stainback, W. and Stainback, S., 95-122. Baltimore: Paul H. Brookes, 1990.

Villa, R., et al. *Restructuring for Caring and Effective Education: Administrative Strategies for Creating Heterogeneous Schools.* Baltimore: Paul H. Brookes, 1992.

Issues in Education

Ledell, Marjorie, and Arnsparger, Arleen. *How to Deal with Community Criticism of School Change.* Alexandria, VA: Association for Supervision and Curriculum Development, 1993.

National Commission on Excellence in Education. *Nation at Risk: The Full Account.* USA Research Staff (ed.), 1984.

———. *Nation at Risk: The Full Account.* 2nd ed. USA Research Inc. Staff (ed.), 1992.

Rasell, Edith, and Rothstein, Richard, Editors. *School Choice: Examining the Evidence.* Washington, DC: Economic Policy Institute, 1993.

Wortman, Bob, and Matlin, Myna. *Leadership in Whole Language: The Principal's Role.* York, ME: Stenhouse Publishers, 1995.

Language Arts

Atwell, Nancie. *Coming to Know: Writing to Learn in the Middle Grades.* Portsmouth, NH: Heinemann, 1990.

———. *In the Middle: Writing, Reading, and Learning with Adolescents.* Portsmouth, NH: Heinemann, 1987.

Beeler, Terri. *I Can Read! I Can Write! Creating a Print-Rich Environment.* Cypress, CA: Creative Teaching Press, 1993.

Beierle, Marlene, and Lynes, Teri. *Teaching Basic Skills through Literature: A Whole Language Approach for Teaching Reading Skills.* Cypress, CA: Creative Teaching

Press, 1993.

Bird, Lois Bridge. *Becoming a Whole Language School: The Fair Oaks Story.* Katonah, NY: Richard C. Owen Publishers, 1989.

Bromley, Karen. *Journalling: Engagements in Reading, Writing, and Thinking.* New York: Scholastic, 1993.

Buros, Jay. *Why Whole Language?* Rosemont, NJ: Programs for Education, 1991.

Butler, Andrea, and Turbill, Jan. *Towards a Reading-Writing Classroom.* Portsmouth, NH: Heinemann, 1984.

Butler, Dorothy. *Cushla and Her Books.* Boston: The Horn Book, 1980.

Calkins, Lucy M. *The Art of Teaching Writing.* Portsmouth, NH: Heinemann, 1986.

———. *Lessons from a Child: On the Teaching and Learning of Writing.* Portsmouth, NH: Heinemann, 1983.

———. *Living Between the Lines.* Portsmouth, NH: Heinemann, 1990.

Clay, Marie. *Becoming Literate.* Portsmouth, NH: Heinemann, 1991.

———. *Observing Young Readers.* Portsmouth, NH: Heinemann, 1982.

———. *Reading Recovery: A Guidebook for Teachers in Training.* Portsmouth, NH: Heinemann, 1993.

Clifford, John. *The Experience of Reading: Louise Rosenblatt and Reader-Response Theory.* Portsmouth, NH: Heinemann, 1991.

Cloonan, Kathryn L. *Sing Me A Story, Read Me a Song* (Books I and II). Beverly Hills, FL: Rhythm & Reading Resources, 1991.

———. *Whole Language Holidays.* (Books I and II). Beverly Hills, FL: Rhythm & Reading Resources, 1992.

Dewey, John. *The Child and the Curriculum* and *The School and Society.* Chicago: Phoenix Books, combined edition, 1956.

Eisele, Beverly. *Managing the Whole Language Classroom: A Complete Teaching Resource Guide for K-6 Teachers.* Cypress, CA: Creative Teaching Press, 1991.

Fairfax, Barbara, and Garcia, Adela. *Read! Write! Publish!* Cypress, CA: Creative Teaching Press, 1992.

Fisher, Bobbi. *Joyful Learning: A Whole Language Kindergarten.* Portsmouth, NH: Heinemann, 1991.

Goodman, Yetta. *How Children Construct Literacy.* Newark, DE: International Reading Association, 1990.

Goodman, Yetta M.; Hood, Wendy J.; and Goodman, Kenneth S. *Organizing for Whole Language.* Portsmouth, NH: Heinemann, 1991.

Graves, Donald. *Build a Literate Classroom.* Portsmouth, NH: Heinemann, 1991.

———. *A Researcher Learns to Write.* Portsmouth, NH: Heinemann, 1984.

Haack, Pam, and Merrilees, Cynthia. *Ten Ways to Become a Better Reader.* Cleveland, OH: Modern Curriculum Press, 1991.

Hall, Nigel, and Robertson, Anne. *Some Day You Will No All About Me: Young Children's Explorations in the World of Letters.* Portsmouth, NH: Heinemann, 1991.

Holdaway, Don. *The Foundations of Literacy.* New York: Scholastic, 1979.

———. *Stability and Change in Literacy Learning.* Portsmouth, NH: Heinemann, 1984.

Pavelka, Patricia. *Making the Connection: Learning Skills Through Literature (K-2).* Peterborough, NH: Crystal Springs Books, 1995.

———. *Making the Connection: Learning Skills Through Literature (3-6).* Peterborough, NH: Crystal Springs Books, 1997.

Peetboom, Adrian. *Shared Reading: Safe Risks with Whole Books.* Toronto, Ont.: Scholastic TAB, 1986.

Raines, Shirley C., and Canady, Robert J. *Story Stretchers.* Mt. Ranier, MD: Gryphon House, 1989.

———. *More Story Stretchers.* Mt. Ranier, MD: Gryphon House, 1991.

———. *Story Stretchers for the Primary Grades.* Mt. Ranier, MD: Gryphon House, 1992.

Rief, Linda. *Seeking Diversity: Language Arts with Adolescents.* Portsmouth, NH: Heinemann, 1992.

Routman, Regie. *Transitions: From Literature to Literacy.* Portsmouth, NH: Heinemann, 1988.

———. *Invitations: Changing as Teachers and Learners K-12.* Portsmouth, NH: Heinemann, 1991.

———. *Literacy at the Crossroads: Critical Talk About Reading, Writing, and Other Teaching Dilemmas.* Portsmouth, NH: Heinemann, 1996.

Vail, Priscilla. *Common Ground: Whole Language and Phonics Working Together.* Rosemont, NJ: Programs for Education, 1991.

Language Arts — Bilingual

Whitmore, Kathryn F., and Crowell, Caryl G. *Inventing a Classroom: Life in a Bilingual, Whole Language Learning Community.* York, ME: Stenhouse Publishers, 1994.

Language Arts — Spelling and Phonics

Bean, Wendy, and Bouffler, Christine. *Spell by Writing.* Portsmouth, NH: Heinemann, 1988.

Bolton, Faye, and Snowball, Diane. *Ideas for Spelling.* Portsmouth, NH: Heinemann, 1993.

Booth, David. *Spelling Links.* Ontario: Pembroke Publishers, 1991.

Buchanan, Ethel. *Spelling for Whole Language Classrooms.* Winnipeg, Man.: The C.E.L. Group, 1989.

Fry, Edward, Ph.D. *1000 Instant Words.* Laguna Beach, CA: Laguna Beach Educational Books, 1994.

———. *Phonics Patterns: Onset and Rhyme Word Lists.* Laguna Beach, CA: Laguna Beach Educational Books, 1994.

Gentry, J. Richard. *My Kid Can't Spell.* Portsmouth, NH: Heinemann, 1996.

———. *Spel . . . Is a Four-Letter Word.* New York: Scholastic, 1987.

Gentry, J. Richard, and Gillet, Jean Wallace. *Teaching Kids to Spell.* Portsmouth, NH: Heinemann, 1993.

Lacey, Cheryl. *Moving on in Spelling: Strategies and Activities for the Whole Language Classroom.* New York: Scholastic, 1994.

Powell, Debbie, and Hornsby, David. *Learning Phonics and Spelling in a Whole Language Classroom.* New York: Scholastic, 1993.

Trisler, Alana, and Cardiel, Patrice. *My Word Book.* Rosemont, NJ: Modern Learning Press, 1994.

———. *Words I Use When I Write.* Rosemont, NJ: Modern Learning Press, 1989.

———. *More Words I Use When I Write.* Rosemont, NJ: Modern Learning Press, 1990.

Wagstaff, Janiel. *Phonics That Work! New Strategies for the Reading/Writing Classroom.* New York: Scholastic, 1995.

Wittels, Harriet, and Greisman, Joan. *How to Spell It.* New York: Putnam, 1982.

Learning Centers

Cook, Carole. *Math Learning Centers for the Primary Grades.* West Nynack, NY: The Center for Applied Research in Education, 1992.

Ingraham, Phoebe Bell. *Creating and Managing Learning Centers: A Thematic Approach.* Peterborough, NH: Crystal Springs Books, 1996.

Isbell, Rebecca. *The Complete Learning Center Book.* Beltsville, MD: Gryphon House, 1995.

Poppe, Carol A., and Van Matre, Nancy A. *Language Arts Learning Centers for the Primary Grades.* West Nynack, NY: The Center for Applied Research in Education, 1991.

———. *Science Learning Centers for the Primary Grades.* West Nynack, NY: The Center for Applied Research in Education, 1985.

Wait, Shirleen S. *Reading Learning Centers for the Primary Grades.* West Nynack, NY: The Center for Applied Research in Education, 1992.

Waynant, Louise, and Wilson, Robert M. *Learning Centers: A Guide for Effective Use.* Paoli, PA: Instructo Corp., 1974.

Learning Styles/Multiple Intelligences

Armstrong, Thomas. *In Their Own Way: Discovering and Encouraging Your Child's Personal Learning Style.* New York: Putnam, 1987.

———. *Learning Styles: Food for Thought and 130 Practical Tips for Teachers K-4.* Rosemont, NJ: Modern Learning Press, 1992.

———. *Multiple Intelligences in the Classroom.* Alexandria, VA: Association for Supervision and Curriculum Development, 1994.

———. *Seven Kinds of Smart: Identifying and Developing Your Many Intelligences.* New York: A Plume Book, 1993.

Banks, Janet Caudill. *Creative Projects for Independent Learners.* CATS Publications, 1995.

Bloom, Benjamin S. *All Our Children Learning: A Primer for Teachers and Other Educators.* New York: McGraw-Hill, 1981.

———, ed. *Developing Talent in Young People.* New York: Ballantine, 1985.

Campbell, Bruce. *The Multiple Intelligences Handbook: Lesson Plans and More . . . .* Stanwood, WA: Campbell & Associates, 1994.

Campbell, Linda; Campbell, Bruce; and Dickinson, Dee. *Teaching & Learning Through Multiple Intelligences.* Needham Heights, MA: Allyn & Bacon, 1996.

Carbo, Marie. *Reading Styles Inventory Manual.* Roslyn Heights, New York: National Reading Styles Institute, 1991.

Carbo, Marie; Dunn, Rita; and Dunn, Kenneth. *Teaching Students to Read Through Their Individual Learning Styles.* Needham Heights, MA: Allyn & Bacon, 1991.

Gardner, Howard. *Frames of Mind: The Theory of Multiple Intelligences.* New York: Basic Books, 1985.

———. *Multiple Intelligences: The Theory in Practice.* New York: Basic Books, 1990.

———. *The Unschooled Mind: How Children Think and How Schools Should Teach.* New York: Basic Books, 1990.

Gilbert, Labritta. *Do Touch: Instant, Easy Hands-on Learning Experiences for Young Children.* Mt. Ranier, MD: Gryphon House, 1989.

Grant, Janet Millar. *Shake, Rattle and Learn: Classroom-Tested Ideas That Use Movement for Active Learning.* York, ME: Stenhouse Publishers, 1995.

Lazear, David. *Multiple Intelligence Approaches to Assessment: Solving the Assessment Conundrum.* Palatine, IL: IRI/Skylight Publishing, Inc., 1994.

———. *Seven Pathways of Learning: Teaching Students and Parents About Multiple Intelligences.* Tucson, AZ: Zephyr Press, 1994.

———. *Seven Ways of Knowing: Teaching for Multiple Intelligences.* Palatine, IL: IRI/Skylight Publishing, Inc., 1991.

———. *Seven Ways of Teaching: The Artistry of Teaching With Multiple Intelligences.* Palatine, IL: IRI/Skylight Publishing, Inc., 1991.

New City School Faculty. *Celebrating Multiple Intelligences: Teaching for Success.* St. Louis, MO: The New City School, Inc., 1994.

Vail, Priscilla. *Gifted, Precocious, or Just Plain Smart.* Rosemont, NJ: Programs for Education, 1987.

———. *Learning Styles: Food for Thought and 130 Practical Tips for Teachers K-4.* Rosemont, NJ: Modern Learning Press, 1992.

Multiage Education

American Association of School Administrators. *The Nongraded Primary: Making Schools Fit Children.* Arlington, VA, 1992.

Anderson, Robert H., and Pavan, Barbara Nelson. *Nongradedness: Helping It to Happen.* Lancaster, PA: Technomic Press, 1992.

Banks, Janet Caudill. *Creating the Multi-age Classroom.* Edmonds, WA: CATS Publications, 1995.

Bingham, Anne A.; Dorta, Peggy; McClasky, Molly; and O'Keefe, Justine. *Exploring the Multiage Classroom.* York, ME: Stenhouse Publishers, 1995.

Davies, Anne; Politano, Colleen; and Gregory, Kathleen. *Together is Better.* Winnipeg, Canada: Peguis Publishers, 1993.

Gaustad, Joan. "Making the Transition From Graded to Nongraded Primary Education." *Oregon School Study Council Bulletin,* 35(8), 1992.

———. "Nongraded Education: Mixed-Age, Integrated and Developmentally Appropriate Education for Primary Children." *Oregon School Study Council Bulletin,* 35(7), 1992.

———. "Nongraded Education: Overcoming Obstacles to Implementing the Multiage Classroom." *Oregon School Study Council Bulletin,* 38(3,4), 1994.

Goodlad, John I., and Anderson, Robert H. *The Nongraded Elementary School.* New York: Teachers College Press, 1987.

Grant, Jim, and Johnson, Bob. *A Common Sense Guide to Multiage Practices.* Columbus, OH: Teachers' Publishing Group, 1995.

Grant, Jim; Johnson, Bob; and Richardson, Irv. *Multiage Q&A: 101 Practical Answers to Your Most Pressing Questions.* Peterborough, NH: Crystal Springs Books, 1995.

———. *Our Best Advice: The Multiage Problem Solving Handbook.* Peterborough, NH: Crystal Springs Books, 1996.

Grant, Jim, and Richardson, Irv, compilers. *Multiage Handbook: A Comprehensive Resource for Multiage Practices.* Peterborough, NH: Crystal Springs Books, 1996.

Maeda, Bev. *The Multi-Age Classroom.* Cypress, CA: Creative Teaching Press, 1994.

Miller, Bruce A. *Children at the Center: Implementing the Multiage Classroom.* Portland, OR: Northwest Regional Educational Laboratory; 1994.

———. *The Multigrade Classroom: A Resource Handbook for Small, Rural Schools.* Portland, OR: Northwest Regional Educational Laboratory, 1989.

———. *Training Guide for the Multigrade Classroom: A Resource for Small, Rural Schools.* Portland, OR: Northwest Regional Educational Laboratory, 1990.

Ostrow, Jill. *A Room With a Different View: First Through Third Graders Build Community and Create Curriculum.* York, ME: Stenhouse Publishers, 1995.

Politano, Colleen, and Davies, Anne. *Multi-Age and More.* Winnipeg, Canada: Peguis Publishers, 1994.

Rathbone, Charles; Bingham, Anne; Dorta, Peggy; McClaskey, Molly; and O'Keefe, Justine. *Multiage Portraits: Teaching and Learning in Mixed-age Classrooms.* Peterborough, NH: Crystal Springs Books, 1993.

Stone, Sandra J. *Creating the Multiage Classroom.* Glenview, IL: GoodYear Books, 1996.

Virginia Education Association and Appalachia Educational Laboratory. *Teaching Combined Grade Classes: Real Problems and Promising Practices.* Charleston, WV: Appalachian Educational Laboratory, 1990.

Parent Involvement / Resources for Parents

Baskwill, Jane. *Parents and Teachers: Partners in Learning.* Toronto, Ont.: Scholastic, 1990.

Bettelheim, Bruno. *A Good Enough Parent.* New York: Alfred A. Knopf, 1987.

Butler, Dorothy, and Clay, Marie. *Reading Begins at Home.* Portsmouth, NH: Heinemann, 1982.

Clay, Marie. *Writing Begins at Home.* Portsmouth, NH: Heinemann, 1988.

Coletta, Anthony. *Kindergarten Readiness Checklist for Parents.* Rosemont, NJ: Modern Learning Press, 1991.

Elovson, Allanna. *The Kindergarten Survival Handbook.* Santa Monica, CA: Parent Ed Resources, 1991.

Grant, Jim. *Jim Grant's Book of Parent Pages.* Rosemont, NJ: Programs for Education, 1988.

Grant, Jim, and Azen, Margot. *Every Parent's Owner's Manuals. (Three-, Four-, Five-, Six-, Seven-Year- Old).* Rosemont, NJ. Programs for Education. 16 pages each manual.

Henderson, Anne T.; Marburger, Carl L.; and Ooms, Theodora. *Beyond the Bake Sale: An Educator's Guide to Working with Parents.* Columbia, MD: National Committee for Citizens in Education, 1990.

Hill, Mary. *Home: Where Reading and Writing Begin.* Portsmouth, NH: Heinemann, 1995.

Karnofsky, Florence, and Weiss, Trudy. *How to Prepare Your Child for Kindergarten.* Carthage, IL: Fearon Teacher Aids, 1993.

Lazear, David. *Seven Pathways of Learning: Teaching Students and Parents About Multiple Intelligences.* Tucson, AZ: Zephyr Press, 1994.

Lyons, P.; Robbins, A.; and Smith, A. *Involving Parents: A Handbook for Participation in Schools.* Ypsilanti, MI: High/Scope Press, 1984.

Vopat, James. *The Parent Project: A Workshop Approach to Parent Involvement.* York, ME: Stenhouse Publishers, 1994.

Team Teaching

Erb, Thomas O., and Doda, Nancy M. *Team Organization: Promise—Practices and Possibilities.* Washington, D.C.: National Education Association of the United States, 1989.

Northern Nevada Writing Project Teacher-Researcher Group. *Team Teaching.* York, ME: Stenhouse Publishers, 1996.

Themes

Atwood, Ron, ed. *Elementary Science Themes: Change Over Time; Patterns; Systems and Interactions; Models and Scales.* Lexington, KY: Institute on Education Reform, University of Kentucky, 1993. Set of four pamphlets, 50 pages each.

Bromley, Karen; Irwin-De Vitis, Linda; and Modlo, Marcia. *Graphic Organizers: Visual Strategies for Active Learning.* New York: Scholastic, 1995.

Davies, Anne; Politano, Colleen; and Cameron, Caren. *Making Themes Work.* Winnipeg, Canada: Peguis Publishers, 1993.

Gamberg, Ruth; Kwak, W.; Hutchins, R.; and Altheim, J. *Learning and Loving It: Theme Studies in the Classroom.* Portsmouth, NH: Heinemann, 1988.

Haraway, Fran, and Geldersma, Barbara. *12 Totally Terrific Theme Units.* New York: Scholastic, 1993.

Herr, Judy, and Libby, Yvonne. *Creative Resources for the Early Childhood Classroom.* Albany, NY: Delmar, 1990.

Katz, Lilian G., and Chard, Sylvia C. *Engaging Children's Minds: The Project Approach.* Norwood, NJ: Ablex Press, 1989.

McCarthy, Tara. *150 Thematic Writing Activities.* New York: Scholastic, 1993.

McCracken, Marlene and Robert. *Themes.* (9 book series). Winnipeg, Man.: Peguis Publishers, 1984-87.

SchifferDanoff, Valerie. *The Scholastic Integrated Language Arts Resource Book.* New York: Scholastic, 1995.

Schlosser, Kristin. *Thematic Units for Kindergarten.* New York: Scholastic, 1994.

Strube, Penny. *Theme Studies, A Practical Guide: How to Develop Theme Studies to Fit Your Curriculum.* New York: Scholastic, 1993.

Thompson, Gare. *Teaching Through Themes.* New York: Scholastic, 1991.

Index

About the Authors

Char Forsten is a national lecturer and instructor on looping and multiage practices, as well as mathematics and other topics of interest to elementary educators. She leads customized training seminars for schools, helping them to set up and implement looping and multiage programs. She also facilitates the change process in schools. Char has 18 years of classroom experience, including fifteen at the Dublin Consolidated School in Dublin, New Hampshire, where she acted as teaching principal for six of those years. She holds a Bachelor of Science degree in Elementary Education from Pennsylvania State University and an MBA from Plymouth State College. She is the author of *The Multiyear Lesson Plan Book, Using Calculators Is Easy, Teaching Thinking and Problem Solving in Math,* and *Cobblestone Companion.* She currently presents on many educational topics for The Society For Developmental Education.

Jim Grant is the founder and executive director of The Society For Developmental Education. He has been, for the past seven years, the primary advocate for both looping and multiage education, lecturing nationwide on these topics as well as on developmental education, readiness issues, and retention. He is the founder of the National Alliance of Multiage Educators (N.A.M.E.). He was a teaching multiage principal for over twenty years before beginning his career in teacher training. He is the author of several books, including *The Looping Handbook: Students and Teachers Progressing Together, Retention and Its Prevention: Making Informed Decisions About Individual Children, I Hate School!, Developmental Education in the 1990s, Multiage Q&A: 101 Practical Answers to Your Most Pressing Questions, A Common Sense Guide to Multiage Practices,* and *Our Best Advice: The Multiage Problem Solving Handbook.*